P9-DEY-254

TO HONOR A TEACHER

TO HONOR A TEACHER

Students Pay Tribute to Their Most Influential Mentors

Collected by

JEFF SPODEN

Andrews McMeel Publishing

Kansas City

www.andrewsmcmeel.com
Book design by Susan Hood

Library of Congress Cataloging-in-Publication Data
To honor a teacher : students pay tribuute to their most influential mentors / collected by Jeff Spoden.
   p. cm.
  ISBN 0-7407-0051-0
  1. Teacher-student relationships—United States. 2. Teachers—United States—Anecdotes. I. Spoden, Jeff.
LB1033.T6 1999
371 102′3′0973—dc21   99-22164
                                    CIP

*T*hank you to _____

_____

_____

_____

_____

_____

_____

_____

_____

_____

Signed

I dedicate this book to the inspiring
teachers who will touch the lives of my
children, Sarah and Sam. I thank them in advance,
and hope that one day their stories will also be told.

And to Stephanie, my most gifted sage,
for trying to teach me how to parent with respect
and to love with honesty and an open heart.

CONTENTS

FOREWORD

This book is a tribute to teachers. In the largest sense, of course, we are all teachers. Good parents teach their children to talk and feed themselves and socialize, as they teach them to be moral and kind. Wise shopkeepers teach customers ethics as well as product discernment. Hairstylists teach the art of conversation at the same time that they demonstrate hair care. As we watch each other, and pass each other, and interact with each other, we are, by our very being, teaching each other ways to be. This is surely the most fundamental lesson we need to learn, and we do it naturally, as if by osmosis.

Pedagogy is different. I think of it as the art of passing on to others—individually or in groups—special skills or particular information that would not get passed on in the normal course of life. How to read. Geography. Square dancing. Playing the saxophone. Cardiopulmonary resuscitation. I know it's possible to teach oneself by reading—my cousin Andy taught himself to play saxophone by reading books and listening to records, but eventually, for his playing to be inspired, he needed to find a teacher.

My experience has been that information passes between people—skills learning happens—on two wavelengths. One is the level of information. The other is the level of emotional charge. The best learning happens, I think, when the student senses, *This material is important to this person. This teacher cares about this.*

A few years into my mindfulness practice, years in which I was happily attending retreats and enjoying hearing what the Buddha taught, but not being zealous in my meditation practice, I had an interview (routine for students on retreat) with James Baraz, one of the teachers. I described to James some small moment of awakened attention I'd experienced, and he said, eagerly leaning forward and speaking with eloquent urgency, "That's very good. Now be sure to watch even *more* closely to see what happens next!" I was struck by his sincerity, his clear excitement that I might get to share what he knew to be the great benefits of mindfulness. I immediately changed my practice. I became zealous. (Thank you, James.) I had known before that moment that James liked me, that he cared about me. But that he cared so much about mindfulness, about what he was teaching, spoke to me deeply.

I think the best teachers have—in addition to mastery of their information and a passion for their subject—an inner imperative for passing information on to others. I think of it as a "teaching gene." My father had it. I inherited it from him. Its manifestation is an inner mandate—arising from the delight in whatever it is one knows—to find someone to teach it to. I love to teach. The pleasure I feel when I explain something, and someone else really understands it, is thrilling.

There is a story about a Zen teacher who achieved his enlightenment when he was sixty years old. Accounts say he then waited twenty years, consolidating his insight, before he taught it. Sometimes I am chagrined to realize that I wait perhaps twenty *minutes* before I try to teach something I've just learned that excites me. The Zen master lived in another culture, and when he died, he was a very, very old man. For all the rest of us, now, who are blessed with a teaching gene and a skill we love, may we begin soon and teach long and passionately and carefully, with as much wisdom as we can.

This book is a tribute to today's teachers and an inspiration to teachers of the future.

Sylvia Boorstein

PREFACE

I love being a teacher, though it is not my first occupational choice. I'd rather be point guard for the Los Angeles Lakers, or a justice of the United States Supreme Court, or—surprise—a rock star. The reality, however, is that I'm forty-three years old, I can't sing or play an instrument, I was tenth man on my high school frosh/soph basketball team, and I could write a book much longer than this about why I'll never be on the Supreme Court.

So for this lifetime, I'm stuck with my fourth and most practical career option, teaching. Fortunately, I love the job. I love getting up each morning knowing I will touch someone's life, either intellectually or emotionally. I love knowing each and every day at least one of my students will have gained from contact with me. I love being part of a profession whose practitioners can collectively leave their buildings on Friday afternoon, having had the opportunity to

Help young people learn
Teach facts
Teach skills

Teach them to find their own facts and develop their own skills
Teach them to solve their own problems
Foster interest and curiosity
Help develop and clarify career goals
Stimulate ideas
Push both intellectual and physical limits
Support
Counsel
Encourage creativity
Provide a safe environment for productive social interaction
Befriend
Challenge
Empower
Aid in the exploration of personal and social values
Help to make sense of the modern information barrage
Promote citizenship
Coach
Promote growth from setbacks and failure
Spawn dreams
Mend
Create opportunities
Listen

In essence, to lay a foundation upon which young people's lives will be constructed and reconstructed for a lifetime.

How many people can say this? How many can assume that every single working day will bring growth to the life of at least one and probably many more young people?

But having said this, and firmly believing it, I must admit to a frustration built into the fiber of my profession. We hope to accomplish some or all of the above, but given the abstract nature of human growth, we rarely experience success concretely. How do we, as teachers, really know what our impact is? How do we measure success in the above endeavors? Helping a young man through a difficult period of his life or opening up a sixteen-year-old girl to new ideas and ways of analyzing the world is not a quantifiable achievement.

In many professions, the product of one's labor is tangible. The architect drives by a home or building of her design; an artist has his paintings, a ballplayer his career statistics; a doctor knows when her patient gets well and a lawyer either wins a case or loses it; engineers and construction workers combine to create a Golden Gate Bridge; a CEO posts a well-scrutinized profit or loss for each fiscal year. These results are in some way concrete—they can be measured, touched, tasted, walked on, driven over, stared at, lived in, put on the wall, and clapped for.

Then there are teachers, the professionals who can rightly claim a small piece of every student's accomplishment, be it open-heart surgery or striking out a batter with runners on in the bottom of the ninth, but who hold little tangible evidence of their own impact. The high school drafting teacher rarely knows it was her student who designed the beautiful building she drives by. The fifth-grade teacher, whose energy cultivated curiosity, uniqueness, and love of color in a budding little painter, will never see the slight trace of his own stroke reflected in the artist's canvas.

Certainly there are small victories each week, such as an outstanding paper, a student finally understanding a tough equation, or a class slowly and thoughtfully drilling its way to the deeper depths of a discussion topic. And there are, year after year, the changes we see in students from September to June, as they acquire new skills, ideas, interests, and maturity. Still, we must wonder how much of this student achievement would have taken place in our absence. We wonder if another teacher could have done it just as well; we wonder whether we, personally, made a significant contribution to this young person's life. For me, this always shakes down to two questions: Do I have a lasting legacy? Do I offer anything that these students carry out into the world and use for their own good, and for the good of others?

I have a sense that I do, but only because at the end of each year, I create an avenue for students to tell me what I've meant to them. I purchase a yearbook along with twelve hundred student buyers and ask my own students to sign it. Through these signatures, I learn some things I never would have guessed or imagined or hoped.

I distinctly remember the last day of school, June 1993, sitting in my classroom. I had been fighting a debilitating illness for two months and had clung to both my teaching and my self-esteem by jagged fingernails. I hadn't taught my students a stitch of history since March and didn't feel much like a teacher. Since so much of my identity is wrapped up in my job, that meant not feeling like anything at all. I sat at my desk, gazing toward an upper corner of the room with what must have been a pensive expression, pale, thin, and utterly worn out. I actually thought of

Sidney Poitier in *To Sir with Love:* teacher sitting alone at his desk, slightly dazed from having said good-bye to young people with whom he had shared a room and a life, but whom, with few exceptions, he'd never see again.

I picked up the yearbook on my desk and started to read.

Mr. Spoden,
Our lives are reflections of our minds, and society, of our collected consciousness. The Master of Huai-nan once said, "It takes more than one wise man to correct the ills of a chaotic society." Although you are a great sage, you cannot correct everything all alone. Therefore, the fact that you are a teacher, helping others learn to save our world, is all the more important. Thank you for everything.

Trevor Getz

The tears these words drew from me brought months of frustration and anguish into my hands. For some students, I had still managed to be a teacher.

I'm healthy again, trying to maintain an energetic, stimulating style of instruction. But I gratefully acknowledge that my yearbooks helped pull me through that crisis and many other minor slumps. Every year I pull a few of the books off my shelf and read what students have said about their experiences in my class. I'm always profoundly moved and, out of loyalty to the nagging self-critic inside, profoundly surprised. Are these comments really about me? Hmmm?

This is not to imply that teachers should become praise

junkies, currying "warm fuzzies" from students and casting them as shrines to their success. Teachers who want to be liked more than they want to educate don't last. This is why I've known very few teachers in my life who fit into this category. My colleagues care far more about professional integrity than about strokes from students. We do this job out of love for young people, and love for ideas, creativity, exploration, and fun, not out of some craving for pats on the back.

But, but, but, but, but! It's still nice to be appreciated. It's still nice to get feedback that helps us understand what we have given this creature called "student." I fully understood this contradiction between wanting to be thanked and not needing to be last year when I turned over my classes to a student teacher. One of my students wrote me a beautiful letter expressing his disappointment at my leaving the class.

I was deeply moved, but his letter's effect was subtle. I dragged myself out of bed at 5:45 the next morning, hated the world for about twenty minutes, warmed up over breakfast to the idea of existence, actually looked forward to going to work by 7:00, went to school, and taught my classes no differently than I had the day before. I didn't need his letter to make me feel good about myself or to motivate me to be a good teacher that specific Wednesday. But I was a different person. I had been changed, as one must be changed, by the enormity of having impacted a young life. Deeply, imperceptibly; in my blood, an almost spiritual mix of pride and gratitude that keeps me dedicated to doing the best I can for other people's kids. So, paradoxically, in taking the time and risk to let me know how he felt, this student gave me a gift that was both unnecessary and utterly priceless.

It is in the spirit of this young man's letter and my yearbooks that *To Honor a Teacher* has been born. Teachers may never be able to point to concrete artifacts of their labors, but the appreciative testimonies of current or former students offer them glimpses of their lasting significance. Here are stories and poems by people from all walks of life about teachers, mentors, and coaches who have been important. These stories tend not to be of the gut-wrenching "I was going to commit suicide until a stranger came up to me and smiled" variety. They lack, as one disinterested literary agent politely pronounced, a certain commercially viable "pith and punch." Rather, these are simple stories about everyday working heroes who shape lives in nine-month chunks.

To the givers of this book, thank you. To its recipients, you deserve it. To everyone, please do the following: Give this book to a teacher, mentor, or coach of your own.

If you don't give them the book, tell them, in some way, how significant they have been to you.

If you don't know where they are, find them. Submit your own MIT (Most Influential Teacher!) story or poem to the Teacher Appreciation Project (see page 229). Enjoy *To Honor a Teacher*.

Jeff Spoden
Director, Teacher Appreciation Project

ACKNOWLEDGMENTS

It seems impossible to thank everyone who deserves my gratitude. So many people have helped in so many ways. Thanks to:

Larry Sydes for his ongoing interest and encouragement. As an independent bookseller for the past years, he has always insisted there is a market for this book.

Paul Dalmas and Vicki Hackett for valuable comments on pieces I wrote for the book.

Julie Wong, with whom I exchanged high-energy e-mails early in the process. Some nights this electronic correspondence kept me glued to my computer, a wild-eyed insomniac who believed this project wouldn't fade away.

Marc Polonsky, who kicked around ideas with me, got angry when I forgot that my work was no more important than his, did days of first-draft editing, fought with me when I didn't uphold my end of the bargain, helped me make the most difficult decision of the entire process, and through it all, stayed my friend.

Amy Friedman Fraser, without whom this work would still be lodged in the middle of a manuscript stack of some overworked acquisitions editor. She saved me from a year of frustration and headaches.

Mike Parsons for having the good sense to want to teach and for showing up at Northgate just when I needed to pump life back into a deflated undertaking. It won't be long before he is written about in a book like this.

My mom, for belief, encouragement, and typing.

Ginny Gagne for her typing of tributes.

Dr. Jane Bluestein for her generous help and support.

Thanks to all the people who contributed parts of the book that ultimately weren't included: Lynda Chittenden, Gail Emery, Suzy Kohl, Susan Luzzaro, Mike Messner, Ralph Opacic, Debbie Steinberg, Peter Steinberg, and Deborah Straw for essays; Tamsen Dunn for her beautiful illustrations; Christine Davis, Juan Montalvo, Rich Schwerin, and Gina Tonti for some excellent photographs.

To Linda Bland, my editor and agent, to whom thanks is pitifully inadequate. The reality is that her name should be on the book's cover right beside my own. She took a rough beauty and really made it glow. She also guided me through an unknown world in a way that truly defined professionalism.

To my wife, Stephanie, who was my greatest supporter and most honest critic. She made me understand that the project wasn't done just because I wanted it to be; she helped me with every aspect of the book development; and, though at times it made me angry, she forced me to keep both my motives and priorities rooted in the real world.

Gratitude to Old Teachers

When we stride or stroll across the frozen lake,
We place our feet where they have never been.
We walk along the unwalked. But we are uneasy.
Who is down there but our old teachers?

Water that once could take no human weight—
We were students then—holds up our feet,
And goes ahead of us for a mile.
Beneath us the teachers, and around us the stillness.

—Robert Bly

CHAPTER 1

THE HEALER

*About those who offered comfort
and assurance*

We expect teachers to handle teenage pregnancy,
substance abuse, and the failing of the family.
Then we expect them to educate our children.

—John Sculley

DIANE PAYNE
special education teacher

— writing about —

MRS. PRINS
her third-grade teacher

THE OTHER MOTHER

"Hey, Mrs. Prins!" I shout while waving at her kitchen window. Standing on top of the monkey bars, I stretch across the school boundary fence toward her house, waving frantically, but she doesn't seem to notice. Her husband does though. He closes the kitchen curtains.

Mrs. Prins is my third-grade teacher, though sometimes I accidentally call her "Mom." I know she isn't my mother, but I can't stop hoping she will adopt me if my mother dies. Mrs. Prins knows nothing of this hope, but she knows I like her enough to fight the kids after school who make fun of her curled-up mouth. Half her mouth is always smiling because she had a nerve operation and kids sit at their desks curling up half their mouths, mocking Mrs. Prins behind her back.

As I hang off the monkey bars, I can't understand why Mr. Prins closed the kitchen curtains on me. This makes about as much sense as the kids teasing Mrs. Prins. Maybe he didn't see me hanging off the bars, waving five feet from their window. Through their living room curtains, I can see Mrs. Prins sitting on her couch reading the paper. I start waving and shouting hello again. Mr. Prins walks over and closes those drapes. Now I know he finds me a nuisance.

With all their drapes tightly closed, I remain on the monkey bars in the empty playground, dreading going home, wishing Mr. Prins didn't find me a pest. If *he* wasn't there, Mrs. Prins would invite me over. Just because school is over for the day, *she* can't suddenly find me a pest.

On the first day of school, Mrs. Prins asked me, "Aren't you the girl who used to have that pretty long hair?" I didn't know her yet and was worried about why she had noticed me. Before school started, I had cut my hair off to make sure one more year wouldn't be spent with a cruel teacher yanking it every time I did something wrong. Now all my hair rests in a paper bag in Mom's dresser drawer, safe from cruel teachers. Standing on the monkey bars and short-haired, I imagine what it would be like to have Mrs. Prins brush my long hair while sitting next to her on the couch. But there is no more hair and the drapes are pulled.

As the sky darkens, Mrs. Prins walks into her yard and offers me a few peanut butter cookies and a glass of milk. Instead of walking around the playground, I climb the fence, hoping to impress her with my strength, but she looks worried as I rip my shirt coming down on her side. For once there's no blood, just a torn shirt, not a bruised body.

"Don't you have to go home after school?" she asks.

"Of course, but not right away."

We sit on lawn chairs eating our cookies. Now that I'm finally in her yard, I don't know what to say. "Did you just make these cookies?"

"After school."

"They're the best I ever had," I say, certain she made them especially for me.

When the cookies are finished, I know it's time to walk back home down the half-mile hill. I thank Mrs. Prins for the cookies, leaving her quiet home behind, slowly cutting through the alleys and looking over fences at dogs, wondering if my dad will be home for dinner or at a bar drinking. I feel guilty for having not gone home right away to make dinner, for making Mom have to cook, knowing she's not feeling well. I wonder what Mrs. Prins is having for dinner and figure it won't be frozen fish sticks and a box of macaroni and cheese. That's what we'll be having.

At night I write a story about Pepper, our dog. Mrs. Prins wants the class to write stories about people who are important to us, but it seems like all my important humans would make a sad story. Pepper's different. He's stuck at home, not dying or drinking, just waiting for someone to play with him.

A few days after I hand my story in, Mrs. Prins asks if she can talk with me after school. I agree and then spend the entire day worrying what I did wrong. Three times I go into the bathroom and cry, certain I hurt her feelings by doing something wrong. But after school, Mrs. Prins takes my story out of her desk drawer and asks, "May I keep this story?"

"Why?"

"Because I want to save it in a special drawer at home with all my favorite stories." She looks like she is about to cry and I want to ask for the story back, just to read what I said that could make her feel this way, but I can't speak without crying. Then she hugs me and my eyes swell with tears.

Walking home, I know that even if I never get to sleep in her house, my story does, and that is enough to make Mrs. Prins seem like my mother. This will be my mother, with half a face smiling while the eyes are tearing. The mother I can watch by climbing the monkey bars. And, most importantly, the mother who understands my stories.

PHILLIP ZIEGLER
psychotherapist
— w r i t i n g   a b o u t —
JIM LIVINGSTON
his high school literature teacher

Until my senior year I had terrible grades and hated school. I had been pretty much of a screw-off in high school. I was more interested in getting by with no studying, and hanging out with girls. I heard Prose Fiction was a pretty interesting class and I did like reading fiction. So I signed up for the course.

Jim Livingston's teaching lit a fire under me. He brought his passion for literature to every class. I loved the discussions he always kept lively and fresh. The materials we read were appropriate for our level but also challenging. Over 35 years later I still remember his lectures on the early novel, epistolary novels written as letters, *Pamela, Shamela,* and the works of Jane Austen.

Another thing I loved about Livingston was that he let us know him, how quirky he could be. I remember a story about the dangers of being spontaneous in the wrong place and time. He told us, with great personal openness, about how he was at a University of California football game one time when two guys nearby started to get into a loud argument. Jim, a mild and formal kind of guy, broke out of his usual mode and suddenly shouted, "Hit him!" He was shocked and then utterly dismayed when one guy punched the other and they began fighting like wildcats. I can still see his face: open, innocent, honest, and so human.

He awakened in me a love for learning and for reading that still remains. He demanded that we keep looking deeper into the material and into ourselves. Pretty unusual for 1959. I fell in love with the written word and with fiction. His personal support for me as a troubled but capable student brought me from a sense of inadequacy and failure to a belief that I was bright and competent. He showed me I could excel beyond my performance up to that time.

In my senior year I went from a C and D student to an A student. I completed my senior year—much to the shock of family, friends, and former teachers—on the honor society and as a member of the California Scholarship Federation.

About six months ago I received the Lowell High alumni newspaper and saw a photo of Jim at some event. I wrote to him, care of the high school, and got a letter back about a month later.

I wrote to let him know he was a great teacher, that he had a profound influence on me. And that since his class I have remained a lover of literature. I even married a novelist and poet. He wrote back thanking me and said my letter was now among his prized possessions.

PERMISSION TO SPEAK

As a child I had a terrible stammer, which worsened as adolescence came with its hormonal stresses and changes. I could not pronounce a vowel without a machine-gun stutter of repetition. "Aa-aa-aa-apple," I would say. "Or-or-or-orange," I would splutter. A bright child, I often answered a question—taking pains in word order and placement of consonants—only to find to my chagrin there was a follow-up question I had not anticipated. Here's an example that happened one day:

"Can anyone tell us who was the most important Catholic philosopher? Yes, Michael?"

"That would be the philosopher Thomas—*watch the A coming up*—Thomas S'Aguinas. He was the—*change author for*—writer who gave us the *Summa Theologica*."

"Very good, Michael. And what was the name of the Greek philosopher who influenced him?"

"Ah-ah-ah-eh-eh-ay-aghr-Aristotle!"

I sat down to a chorus of laughs that obliterated my original correct answer and relegated me to the position of class fool. Or worse: an object of pity to Mary Newbury with whom I was desperately in love. I had not told her my feelings, of course, and after this last exhibition, I believed my chances of declaring them and being taken seriously had vanished forever.

One day shortly after this episode my ninth-grade English teacher, Brother Felix, asked me to come see him after my last class. Brother Felix was erasing the blackboard when I entered the room. He told me to have a seat and then he went on to say that when he was a teenager, he used to stutter but that he seldom did anymore.

"How did you get over it?" I asked. He told me he used two tools that were readily available: singing and projecting the voice.

"Do you like to sing?" he asked.

I nodded.

"And I'll bet you don't stutter when you sing; am I right?"

I nodded again.

That week at his suggestion I joined the school choir and began a lifelong passion for music. Even today I sing at Irish gatherings on St. Patrick's Day, I sing Christmas carols each holiday season, I sing in church, and I sing with and to my *own* English classes at the school where I teach. As a poet I reach almost instinctively for the "music" of the line, whether reading the works of another writer or composing my own.

At Brother Felix's suggestion I practiced for Glee Club recitals; I sang solos in the school talent show; I sang high masses in the local Catholic church. I enriched my life in ways I could not have imagined by studies of choral singing, Latin, French, and the history of music. I discovered the music of poetry in Virgil, in Eliot, and in Octavio Paz much earlier and more deeply than I uncovered the meaning.

The skills involved in projecting the voice were harder to learn.

I began after school by shouting memorized speeches and poems to the back of the classroom where Brother Felix sat correcting papers. He was apparently indifferent to my efforts; at the end of the hour, though, he smiled and told me how many lines I had recited without a stammer.

By my sophomore year under his tutelage I had learned gestures, dramatic pauses, voice modulation, and breathing control. I had memorized dozens of poems, speeches, and scenes from plays. I had even begun to write my own scripts and short declamations. By my junior year I had won speech contests across the state, had been on a nationally televised debate tournament, and had given extemporaneous talks in competitions, at Toastmasters, in student legislatures, and at Model United Nations in New York.

I discovered that speaking to large audiences was no more stressful than answering a question in class had been—or asking Mary Newbury for a date. The former I did now with greater frequency; the latter on the occasion of our Junior Prom. Mary accepted with the comment, "Why did you take so long? I liked you when we were in ninth grade!"

Speaking to my graduation class at commencement, I received applause, not laughter or embarrassed silence. Brother Felix showed me that focusing on a weakness with determination and diligence could turn that flaw into a strength. Much of my triumph was due to the intervention of this caring and dedicated teacher.

Brother Felix, long since passed away, is part of who I am and hope to be today. He is with me when I give a poetry reading at the Three Rivers Arts Festival or at the Tequendama Inter-Continental in Bogotá, Colombia. He is with me as I work with my creative writing seminar or my American literature class sharing the passion of writing and the beauty of literature. I will never forget what he gave me on those school-bound afternoons; I try to emulate his example through my own mission as a teacher and a poet. He gave me far more than a tool for dealing with a handicap. He gave me a key to the secret of living fully.

I am still a stammerer, of course. I was simply shown a method wherein I manage to avoid stuttering most of the time, but always the tendency is there. Michael, the ninth-grade student, is forever a part of who I am. When I am sufficiently moved by the language, or by an emotion, a click ascends in the larynx that sometimes is converted into a lilt, a thoughtful pause, a Kennedyesque repetition, or a doubling of the consonant. Other times, as I move to replace one word with another less troubling to the tongue, a dramatic turn in thought or image occurs.

For most people who hear me speak, these devices go unremarked or unnoticed, accepted simply as a wide range of rhetorical devices used by a speaker comfortable with language and ideas. Yet for the part of me that is Michael, the boy in the front row with his hand up, dreading what will come out of his mouth, they are the tools that make me a poet and a teacher today. For the boy in the empty classroom declaiming Patrick Henry's ". . . give me liberty or give me death!" and that boy in the choir transcendent with music, those devices are and always will be the stuff of miracles.

HANNAH FERBER: A THANKS GIVING

The war still lay upon the world
Like a pair of awful hands pressing down,
When Hannah Ferber, Home Room 101,
Entered through the doorway of my life.
She was a Jewess and a refugee, a Ph.D.
Reduced to teaching secretarial skills to girls
Whose higher aspirations were husbands and babies.
But after school in her cluttered apartment
She shared her treasured music:
What shall it be then, girl? she'd ask.
I'd love to hear the Mendelssohn again.
And she would nod and smile and say, *Then you shall!*

The war still floated on the seas
Like a slick of oozing oil spread out,
When Hannah Ferber, teacher to my heart,
Opened the barn doors of my brain.
She was a short and homely sort with thick red hair,
Reduced to wearing dresses almost threadbare,
Outdated shoes and mended runs in her cotton hose.
But after school in her cluttered apartment
She shared her treasured books:
What shall it be then, girl? she'd ask.
I hope you'll read from Eliot again.
And she would nod and smile and say, *Then I shall!*

The war still whistled from the skies
Like flocks of predatory birds diving down,
When Hannah Ferber, teacher to my soul,
First read my little drafts of things and heard me sing.
She was a watchfire, a lantern to my youth,
Reduced to boiling tea on a rusty hotplate
And washing her thick red hair in a dented pan.
But after school in her cluttered apartment
She shared her treasure-self with me:
What will you be then, girl? she asked.
I want to sing and I want to write.
And she nodded and smiled and said, *Then you must!*

June Owens
retired executive secretary,
administrative assistant

GALE OW
social studies teacher

— writing about —

HELEN WONG
her high school teacher

It was a time when Chinese-Americans wanted to believe in assimilation, to blend into the dominant society; we wanted nothing to do with people who looked like us. We were escaping being poor, immigrant, and different. It was the time of Troy Donahue and Sandra Dee; our idols were the Beatles and the Rolling Stones. We wanted to relate to the cultural icons and persons of authority who were of the dominant culture. One thing we did *not* want was Chinese teachers as role models.

In stepped teacher Helen Wong, who was from Chinatown and taught Mandarin. She was just like us, except she was a teacher. I wanted nothing to do with her.

But Helen Wong did not leave me alone. Her class was near my locker and she sensed, being the professional she was, that I was a misguided teenager and a lost soul amidst 660 other students. Still I shunned her and dreaded having to say "hi" to her every day as I passed her room on the way to my locker.

A year passed. Now Helen Wong became my gym teacher. I was so upset that I had to show her respect that I avoided her; I hated the fact she was my teacher. She sensed the tension and left me alone, though not without trying to reach out and convey a sense of caring. In return, I dished out sassiness and a lot of backtalk. I gave her a bad time because I was confused myself and did not know it.

Nine years later was a time of civil rights and ethnic identity. I had just gotten my Master's degree in Sociology and was hoping to teach a Chinese Community Course. The contact person was Helen Wong. I now understood the meaning of self-love and, to our first meeting, wore my Mao Jacket as a symbol of identity.

After all those years, she bore no grudge and continued to reach out and help. She made connections for me to the informational network that is of such importance in such a large institution. She introduced me to her colleagues; she gave me a tour;

she took me to lunch. I felt so guilty. I gave her nothing but grief earlier as her student, yet she found it within herself to forgive and to give again.

Last June, Helen and I met at a community educators' banquet and we were able to reconnect as equals. I was able to thank her for offering a helping hand—and for not giving up on me. Her reply: "The most worthwhile thing we can do with our lives is to give service. Life is purposeful with service." I found myself agreeing with her and that is why I remain a teacher today. She was someone who reached out to me in a way that I now reach out to *my* students. Thank you, Helen, for caring about me, for modeling the educator I came to be.

BARBARA ROUILLARD
special education teacher

— w r i t i n g   a b o u t —

MISS PSILOS
her fourth-grade teacher

Until that September, my mother had been my most beautiful woman, but Miss Psilos beat even her out. My fourth-grade teacher was the most beautiful person I had ever seen: jet black, shoulder-length hair, a slim young body dressed in silk blouses and wool skirts.

As far back as I could remember, I had always wanted to be a teacher; Miss Psilos only strengthened that resolve. She had exquisite jewelry, including a charm bracelet, which I loved to study. Its heavy adornments clanked as she leaned over my desk to correct my work. Miss Psilos always smelled wonderful too.

She taught us many lessons besides academics. Miss Psilos took great pride in her Greek heritage; I wonder if that is why I take such pride in my own ethnic background, French-Canadian.

She did things differently from any teacher I had had before; for example, she ate lunch with us. All the other teachers ate within the secret sanctums of the faculty dining room, savoring a brief respite from their students—something Miss Psilos didn't seem to want or need. I always tried to sit next to her. She taught us table manners, like how to eat "fancy" with your soup spoon. To this day, when I slowly push my spoon away from me through my soup, I think of Miss Psilos every time.

Once our principal, Miss Whitman, yelled at me and I got weepy. Miss Psilos asked me what had happened. I told her Miss Whitman had caught me returning to our empty classroom after school to retrieve my precious Beatle notebook—too valuable to leave in the classroom overnight. As I finished my story, I saw Miss Psilos purse her lips in anger. I loved her so much that day.

Back then no one talked about divorce or welfare or alcoholism or abuse. But there was one student, Paul, who we all knew came from an abusive home; Paul had a father who was a drunkard. One day after lunch, Paul lay his head down on his desk. He was crying.

"Why are you crying, Paul?" Miss Psilos asked him when she entered the classroom. "What's wrong?"

"I haven't eaten in two days. My head hurts real bad," Paul

sobbed. Then Miss Psilos did the most amazing thing: She took Paul's hand, brought him to the cafeteria, opened it up (we later found out), and made him lunch. While he ate, she sat with him for almost an hour.

Meanwhile, the class went wild. I sat at my desk thinking about Miss Psilos and Paul. Then I got out of my seat without permission—something I had never done before in my young life. I had no choice, for permission could not be asked. I stood in the doorway and watched for her down the hall.

Finally, I saw them coming. Paul's face was washed and they were holding hands. He was smiling.

The wrath of God or Miss Whitman—the same thing to me then—must have fallen on Miss Psilos that day, for she had broken a cardinal rule of her profession: She had left our class all alone in the room. I knew she got in trouble. Kids always know. Besides, I heard the secretaries talking.

That year I probably learned about Brazil and Abraham Lincoln and long division. I don't remember. The enduring lessons I learned were about showing compassion and taking risks for others, opening yourself up and having strength of conviction. Now thirty years later, I bring lunch for one of my poor students. Sometimes I get in trouble. Always I remember Miss Psilos. And I know my most beautiful woman was right.

DR. ROBERT LIEB
psychotherapist

— w r i t i n g a b o u t —

FATHER RIEGLE
his theology teacher

One might suppose being Jewish could be an impediment to bonding with a clergyman from a different faith, but in fact it was quite the opposite. Father Riegle gave me the feeling my Jewishness was something to be proud of (a feeling I had not yet fully held). He also gave me a unique view into Christianity; he influenced me as a teenager to read a great deal on Christian theology, and to this day I am fascinated by it.

Dr. Riegle (as he was also titled) was my philosophy and theology teacher in eleventh and twelfth grades. He was also the Episcopalian priest at the private school I attended. He was a beautifully spiritual man who challenged me with the Big Questions in life—questions about God, values, meaning, and purpose.

Because my father died when I was seventeen, those teenage years were very difficult for me. Certainly I had a great deal of "father hunger" that Father Riegle fulfilled. But beyond that, he made me feel that the higher part of my self was fully seen and valued by another person. He was my teacher at a time when I needed to feel I was more than just my mother's behavior problem. Most adults in my life could not see beyond the hair that grew halfway down my back; Father Riegle let me know there was much more to me than my long hair. His lessons suggested a transformative spirit in life, which made sense of a loss I desperately needed to comprehend.

I entered college as a philosophy major—a direct result of the interest Father Riegle had awakened in me. And while that focus was soon replaced by an interest in psychology, he opened my eyes to the religions of the world in a way that transformed me, taking me to a new level of openness about others' viewpoints that has become a cornerstone of my life and profession.

If I were to see Father Riegle again, I would tell him I hope I am as capable of touching others' lives as he was of touching mine.

TO AN OLD TEACHER, ON HEARING OF THE DEATH OF HER LIFE'S COMPANION

For Miss Morriss

I have just heard Miss Dermott died ten years ago,
that you still grieve, and I am sad for that.
She used to crack a pair of trash can lids together,
shouting, *Chests out, ladies! Straighten up those backs!*

She taught us how to march. You taught us how to love
great poetry. *Ladies, listen to Lord Byron!* you would cry,

Listen to John Donne! And you would clap the *Ten
Great Poets* to your breast, declaiming famous lines.

Ladies, you said, *the most important thing to learn
is how to make a sentence sing.* You told us how,
as a young girl, you climbed a cliff to watch the sun
fall down behind the sea, and listened to the gulls

weep overhead, listened to the wind, and answered
them with poetry. You told us it was then
you understood what you would be. We nodded,
thinking that you meant a teacher, when you meant
that you would never be a wife or mother, never
love a man. You loved a woman well. Now she is gone.
And I would like to sit with you, and reminisce.—
Do you remember how, remember when, remember this?

Do you remember, in your office at the end of term,
you lined your girls up in a row and kissed us
all good-bye? And I was shy, and turned my head,
and you were sad, I think.—Miss Morriss,

when my mother died, and the high winds of grief swept up
the cliff of my abandonment, you rose up unannounced,
straight-backed and thin, one arm flung out, hair slipping
from your steel-gray bun. *Ladies, listen to this line!* you cried.

I could not recall the poet, or the poem, or the import
of that line, and yet for weeks and months I heard
your voice: *So shakes the needle, and so stands the pole.*
It made the pain into a shape that I could hold.

Joanna Scott
writer

EMILY KAO
college student

— w r i t i n g   a b o u t —

MR. WILSON
her fourth-grade teacher

Parents neglect to teach their young children the most
fundamental lesson of all—out of sheer hope that ex-
posing their kids to ethnic diversity in school will do the job. We
all like to think because children are born not knowing about
hatred and bigotry, they naturally accept all other kids. But the
truth is that children learn fast and, like adults, they can be cruel.
They can pick out differences. They can judge and even mistreat
peers because of clothes, color of skin, height, and facial features.
As an Asian-American child, I felt this, and went inward as a
result. I did not know how to assimilate into the sometimes not-
so-friendly playground.

From the time I started school until the fourth grade, I was known as the "shy one," the girl who kept to herself and never raised her hand or volunteered her thoughts. Because I was always so shy, my confidence in my own communication skills and qualities was thwarted by my fear of being recognized as different.

It was not until the fourth grade that I started looking people in the eye, thanks to Mr. Wilson, our fourth-grade teacher at Woodside Elementary School in Concord, California. He was a man whose appearance—great height, large build, and thunderous voice—could intimidate any child. But he was unlike any elementary teacher I had ever had.

Mr. Wilson saw the lonely path I was on, isolated by my racial difference and my inability to socialize with classmates. He helped me forge a new route. Unlike other teachers I had had, Mr. Wilson singled me out and challenged me, not just in my schoolwork, but in front of the class. It's funny how just hearing your own voice echo in a quiet classroom for the first time changes your outlook. This might have been grueling at the time, but I realize now what a difference it made in building the confidence I needed.

Before Mr. Wilson, the things I lacked were support and drive to prove to myself I was not different from other students. Even away from the classroom, he impelled me: He encouraged me to play shortstop in softball. This was the coolest, most valuable position to us fourth graders. I was in the spotlight—and it was okay. Slowly, I began to build social skills and interact with other children.

The real turning point, however, came not in our classroom or on the softball diamond, but on a stage. Mr. Wilson encouraged me to act in my first school play, and it was one of the most memorable and influential experiences of my childhood. All the students were asked to try out for the roles they wanted to play; I was reluctant to even try for a speaking part. It was one week before the tryouts when Mr. Wilson took me aside after class and asked me to try out for "Lady Dorinda," the leading lady role. I was thinking, *Is he kidding? The main character of the entire play? The role with the most lines? The role that demanded a student who was outspoken, confident, and who had to possess stage presence like no other!*

Well, he was the teacher. He was Mr. Wilson. So I practiced my lines day after day at home in front of my patient parents. As I recall my determination, I realize I was not necessarily practicing so hard for myself, but more for Mr. Wilson, who had communicated so much faith in me. A week later, I tackled the butterflies and won the part. Some people may call this favoritism; I would rather call it care.

I did not know it at the time, but Mr. Wilson had changed my life. He had inspired me to value my own culture, as well as to have confidence in relating to *other* people who were different. In my silence, he helped me discover voice; in my fear, he pushed me to courage.

Most of all, Mr. Wilson enabled me to discover my true flair for life.

JAYCIE PHELPS
Olympic Gold Medal gymnast

— w r i t i n g   a b o u t —

MRS. DAILY
her high school English teacher

My most influential teacher was Mrs. Daily, my English teacher at Northwest High School. Mrs. Daily was always upbeat and did everything she could to keep our school fun and keep the kids working together. She was in charge of the "Senate," a group of representatives from each grade who organized activities such as Homecoming and Prom. She did more than anyone else to make the school the best it could be. I respect her a great deal for that.

She taught me in the ninth grade and tutored me in the tenth during the year of the Olympics. Mrs. Daily made a deal with me at the beginning of that year: If I made the U.S. Olympic team, she wouldn't charge me for the tutoring. And she kept her word. She has always followed my progress and still keeps in touch with what I am doing. She was a great teacher and is still a great friend.

Mrs. Daily, I would like to say thank you for being so supportive and understanding. You reduced the stress of school for me when I had to deal with the pressure of the Olympics. I appreciate that and hope to stay in touch always.

RAY SKJELBRED
teacher

—— w r i t i n g   a b o u t ——

ROBERT W. WETTLESON
his English teacher

Robert W. Wettleson, my journalism and newspaper production teacher, was Norwegian (as I am), eccentric, and in love with thinking, reading, honesty, and good manners. In him I discovered a love of teaching and a passion for books. He taught me journalism and I became sports editor for the school paper. But beyond that, he felt he could share some of his reading and ideas with me.

With two family moves during high school, I don't feel I settled into any personal direction until my junior year at Franklin High School in Seattle. I was too shy to be friends with many people. Based on what he must have seen as my curiosity about new ideas, he encouraged me and gave me books that mattered to him, books he thought I would like, books I was ready for. He gave me Ibsen, especially *Peer Gynt,* Thorstein Veblen's *Theory of the Leisure Class,* and Sandburg's volumes on Lincoln. They seemed especially real because they had nothing to do with class. I was hooked. My own budding eccentricities were being observed, acknowledged, and supported by a teacher who simply loved these books and didn't link them to classes, grades, or a "successful" future.

Mr. Wettleson was not a popular teacher with everyone, for he was alternately gentle and raging in class. I clearly remember the day (probably the day of a football game) when some cheerleaders in our class tried to sell a few candy canes (for some cause, probably only mildly noble). The rattling of candy wrappers unnerved him while he was talking to the class. He quietly asked the price of the candy canes, took cash out of his pocket, bought all the candy, dumped them into the wastebasket, then jumped up and down on them.

I don't remember much about the rest of that day except I know he was very angry and had a right to be. I also don't think he should have done what he did. But he was hurt and he might have been feeling old and tired.

He was full of wit and good humor most of the time, but he also expected people to take each other seriously. *He* certainly did. He could be silly but not trivial. His hard glare, his mustache, and his bristly manner all gave him a Mark Twain–like appearance, at least to me. Though he was sometimes excessive, I looked up to him because he looked into human experience with all his heart. I wish I had known him better.

Years later, after he was dead, I used to haunt junk stores every weekend in my endless search for good, inexpensive books. On one of these adventures, I came across a slim volume of Sherwood Anderson's *Horses and Men,* a lovely book that contained one of my favorite stories, "I'm a Fool." I opened it and saw a stamped impression on the flyleaf:

From the Library of R. W. Wettleson

He had done it again! To this day I give away books whenever I can.

WHAT MRS. PENNUCCI DID WHEN THE SIXTH-GRADE CLASS WATCHED BRIAN'S SONG AFTER MY FATHER DIED OF CANCER

Saw the projector light filtering through me
Whispered let's go for a walk
Stood me up in the dark cafeteria
Walked me out between the stares
Filled my stomach with Popsicle
Filled my hand with a volume of Dickinson
Steadied my arm with hers
Gave me something to hang on to

Karen Hart
managing editor for the
Lancaster Times

CHAPTER 2

THE THINKER

*About those who sparked a love
of knowledge*

The teacher is one who makes two ideas grow
where only one grew before.

—*Elbert Hubbard*

freelance writer, retired teacher

—— w r i t i n g   a b o u t ——

MARC FELT
his high school social studies teacher

MAZEL TOV, MAESTRO

When I first entered Marc's class, I'd been on an express train to academic oblivion. A scholastic drifter, I had seen ten schools in twelve years. My meanderings through the winding corridors of America's schools taught me to release just enough mental energy to survive. It was autumn of my senior year, and I lacked collegiate ambition.

I can still see myself leaning on my shiny black '56 Buick convertible in the high school parking lot when my twelfth-grade social studies teacher, Marc Felt, marched toward me. Mini-skirted young women, greasy-haired toughs, and assorted hangers-on split from me like cronies from a defeated politician when they noticed the teacher's determined direction. I don't recall his opening line, but I remember some of his talk: "History lives . . . You're a part of it . . . It must be understood to stop the recurrence of evil . . . Get involved! . . . I expect to hear your opinions in class tomorrow—and every day after that."

The next day in Marc's classroom, he asked, "Anthony, your opinion on the Civil Rights Act?" Dumbfounded, I remained silent. "You, Clete"—he turned to an African-American student—"any opinion?"

"No, none."

"Well, folks, before this year is out, you will have shaped opinions. Things just won't happen without your reacting."

Marc made a deliberate bold attack on my academic apathy. He challenged me; he forced me to examine, to think. Issues took on life. His classroom was a daily, probing drama. He was like the lamplighter of old except his spark was intellectual. He ignited the dormant cinders of curiosity trapped within my soul.

For years I had labored desperately to camouflage my scholastic A's beneath a stylish blanket of black leather jackets, Elvis-style sideburns, pointed shoes, broad ebony belts, and hot rods. None of that clutter, none of that fodder, none of that pretense, succeeded in blurring my mentor's vision of me. He blew my cover, my mask.

I must have appeared a freak, an anomaly to him. Exposure of academic capability terrified me; it was not cool to earn good grades. I despised his habit of returning papers in grade order, from 100% on down; I found his reading, "Anthony 99%," so embarrassing. I wanted closet A's from Marc; once I even dared to request a change in his method of returning our papers. My mentor patiently grinned at my suggestion and continued his dogged pattern of descending order. I was fearful of being exposed in so many ways. I was the same person who felt relieved when the school newspaper failed to mention me as a varsity tennis player. Tennis stars weren't looked up to in my neighborhood.

Marc made us all uncomfortable when he forced us to stand face-to-face with the mirror of truth. Eyeball-to-eyeball, blacks, whites, Asians, were encouraged to discuss apartheid. He expected us to dig and delve to the core of issues. I didn't care about China and

Castro. I was too troubled with adolescence and street survival to care about world problems.

"Tony, any opinion on the North Vietnamese?" Talk about foreshadowing! In a few years, several members of our class would visit Southeast Asia—some never to return.

"Patrice Lamumba?" he asked. I had always preferred talking about the New York Yankees; instead I found myself drifting toward the news media when I heard rumblings of the Middle East, South Africa, and Vietnam. He had successfully chipped away at the citadel of my stubbornness.

Daily my mentor hammered at the same familiar themes. Somehow the lifeless maps that hung limply in our high school classroom were infused with life the moment Marc prodded them with his pointer. We were all aware of the exact locations of Cuba, the Congo, and South Africa after his aggressive pointer summoned them to view.

Still I tried to ignore his attempts to tantalize me with teaching. Annually the high school hosted a student-teacher day. On that day, each teacher selected their best student, presented lesson plans, and observed as that student taught all their classes. I was shocked when Marc selected me his teacher of the day.

"But, sir," I pleaded, "you have honors classes. You teach the smartest kids. Why me?"

"Anthony, honestly . . . search your heart. Do you really think any of them are better qualified than you? If you answer yes, then I'll drop it."

"But, sir . . ."

"No buts. You couldn't answer yes. You're my pick." That was his chancy yet effective way of guiding me toward a teaching career. Had I muffed the opportunity, his plan would have failed. Fortunately, he gambled and won. That one-day student teaching opened my mind to his ideas, his suggestions, his notions of citizenship.

Then just as an invigorating spring day lured me to cut class, inviting me to enjoy our area's beautiful beaches in my black eight-cylinder pearl, Marc stopped me at the schoolhouse gate. I was baffled when he bluntly asked, "Why didn't you apply to any colleges?" He didn't ask where I was headed, beach towel in hand. He didn't ask why I had an entourage of a half-dozen sitting in my car. No, he stared directly at me and demanded an immediate answer. For some reason, I couldn't lie to that man. I took refuge in remaining stolidly silent.

Marc said, "Tony, I want to visit your parents."

Visit my parents! That was out of the question. Why bring them into this? I panicked. Requesting a conference would have been bad enough. I couldn't allow a home visit.

"Sir, my parents work," I fired off.

"That's fine, Anthony. I'm sure they don't work twenty-four hours a day, seven days a week." He paused, then added, "I'll call in the morning to schedule a home visit." Teachers weren't supposed to do things like that.

The following evening, my mother surprised me: She said, "Il Maestro is coming to Sunday dinner." I was speechless. New York's former governor Mario Cuomo often talked of the ethnic self-hate prevalent in Italian-Americans of my generation. Troubled, I wondered, *How and when did they arrange dinner?*

What if he didn't understand my parents' melodious yet broken English? I was bathed in guilt. *Was I ashamed of the two people I loved most in the world?* I was afraid—afraid of what Marc would think of me after seeing my parents.

My teacher visited my home the following Sunday. As he sat in the seat of honor, he toasted in Italian, "Salute!" He savored the pasta, complimented the chef, and suggested, "I usually add Marsala wine to my sauce too." Marc then brought his right index finger, middle finger, and right thumb together, kissed them, and gestured toward the heavens. My parents smiled.

The teacher went into the den with Pop. My father handed him one of those braided, stinking cigars. They spoke of Italy, family, and me. Pretentiousness was alien to both men as their words traveled through time and ethnicity that afternoon. Marc spoke slowly. He spoke excitedly. He sprinkled Italian words like *buòno, vino, and scuòla.* He ate exotic treats I dared not try: escargot. Squid. Pop toasted, "Mazel tov, Maestro!"

Language proved a barrier only in my mind. If Marc had difficulty with my parents' lumbering English, it went unnoticed. He must have read meaning in their animated eyes and easily roused smiles. Finally he stood, looked at them sincerely, and said, "Gràzie." He offered the priceless gift of friendship.

As he walked away, I noticed Pop had given him a bottle of his special homemade wine. So quickly he had become a trusted friend. Sicily taught her children to be wary of strangers. Naturally, I was amazed my immigrant parents instantly and completely trusted this teacher.

I did too, and through initial reluctance, followed him into his profession. Since my senior year in high school, I have participated in three dozen school openings as a student, a teacher, and a board of education trustee. At the start of each school year, I am reminded of my mentor. I never did get to speak to him once I started college; I began to study seriously for the first time. I was too involved to visit him and extend a thank-you. Paradoxically, the ideas he gently sowed bore fruit—and kept me too busy to check in with him.

Marc died prematurely. I found out a year later. I was speechless and shaken by that news. That man, as much as anyone, shaped the "me" of today. He lives in the articles, short stories, and poetry I've published. He lives in the thousands of inquisitive, excited faces I cultivate in the classroom, in the stream of students I've encouraged to enter teaching and other professions. He lives in the young journalists I advised for a score of years. He lives in the flood of children whose minds I have somehow managed to stimulate. He lives in the excited face of a hospitalized student:

"Mr. D, why did you come? A lot of teachers wouldn't visit a kid here—not at a hospital. Especially on a day like this," said the pupil-patient as she reached for my moist umbrella and placed it on the radiator. Her blunt statement flipped my internal switch of reverie. She was right. *Why was I there?* I looked back in time.

I patterned myself after Marc. I realize that now. He lives, not only in me, but in all those I've touched and all that my students' affect. "Thanks from all of us," I muttered, sotto voce.

"Thanks to who, Mr. D?" asked my ill student.

"Oh, sorry. This time you caught your teacher daydreaming."

PETE SEEGER
singer, songwriter, activist

— w r i t i n g a b o u t —

HAROLD LEWIS COOK
his English teacher

My most influential teacher was the poet Harold Lewis Cook. He taught English to us teenagers in the mid-1930s. Learning became an adventure: We'd spend a full three months in class reading one Shakespeare play (*Hamlet, Macbeth,* etc.). What we learned were the subtleties of life and of writing—all with a sense of humor.

Harold Lewis Cook has passed away now. He was the friend of other poets like Edna St. Vincent Millay and Max Eastman.

DANIEL GOLDBLATT
rabbi

— w r i t i n g a b o u t —

BILL GREEN
his college professor

Bill Green was a professor who taught with passion. I met him in an *Introduction to Judaism: Jewish Intellectual History* course and subsequently took six other courses from him. I always looked forward to his class, knowing I would be stimulated and engaged.

What was particularly fascinating about studying religion with Bill Green was that, for most of history, the academic study of religion has been in the hands of "believers," who necessarily lacked distance and critical perspective. Bill's approach was to study the history of religion, the sociology of religion, the psychology of religion, the anthropology of religion, and the philosophy of religion, examining how all these other disciplines bore on the subject. The result was a well-rounded, liberal arts education and a wonderful exposure to a wide range of methodologies and perspectives.

Professor Green was always well prepared and extremely organized. He passed out detailed notes at the beginning of lectures so you could concentrate on what he was saying and capture the nuances of his presentation. Although that first class was an introductory course, Bill warmly invited class participation and was delighted by thoughtful or provocative questions.

In seminar courses, he utilized another effective strategy. Course material was divided into subject headings; each student had to choose two topics. For one, we had to write a research paper, which we then delivered to the class as our teaching segment. For the other subject, we had to critique the paper of another student. This method empowered each of us to be the "teacher" of one topic and the primary respondent for the paper we had chosen to critique. This seminar structure demonstrates how much Bill encouraged us to become involved and invested in our own learning.

He insisted that the papers be grammatically and syntactically free of errors and that we express ourselves clearly and directly. He received a copy of each seminar paper one week before its delivery to class; if there were problems or questions, he helped students answer them. These seminars taught many of us how to read and write critically and effectively; this was a great gift to hotshot college students who came in thinking they already knew everything about such fundamentals. Bill Green was able to help us learn without making us feel deficient or inadequate. He demanded our best work, was appreciative of progress, and always praised improvement. Bill was the kind of teacher who believed in his students and encouraged us to reach beyond what we thought were our limitations. For instance, once when he was invited to give a lecture in the community about a topic we had been studying, he asked if I would like to give the talk in his place. I was deeply flattered, though it was certainly a stretch for me. It was exciting and challenging, and I learned a great deal from the experience.

Bill was a powerful force in shaping my intellect during those formative years. As my mentor, he also took a personal interest in my growth as an individual. He shared his own life experiences and invited me to discuss whatever concerns I had in my life outside of classes.

Bill Green taught me the value of discipline and hard work, not to settle for anything but my best effort, and, most importantly, to ignore the artificial limitations imposed from without and within that got in the way of my ability to dream, set lofty goals, and believe in myself and my own abilities. For all of these life lessons, I will always be grateful.

It was well known around the high school that he and I were bitter enemies; I hated Mr. Besse. Besides not being mature enough to be in his class, I had a reputation for loud, aggressive, disruptive, angry behavior: an all-around badass. I met my match with Mr. Besse. He had zero tolerance, put up with none of my shit, and flunked me in English my sophomore year.

I was assigned again to Mr. Besse my junior year. I tried to get a different teacher, but the school denied me, instead asking me just to behave and all would go well. "Oh sure!" quipped this hellion. The first day of class Mr. Besse pulled me aside and called a truce: If I would sit quietly and give him no trouble, he would in turn pretend I was not there and pass me. Deal. A moron of my word, I sat without interrupting—and began to hear.

I heard Sartre, Shakespeare, Thoreau, to name a few. All of a sudden I *wanted* to participate. I read everything he put in front of us. I always came to class prepared, knew all the answers, was the only student who volunteered. I aced all his tests and quizzes, and when class was over each day, I couldn't wait for it to begin again the next day.

Mr. Besse saw what was going on and encouraged me,

although at times he would not let me participate because he was teaching others as well. But if he could get nothing from them, he would relent and say, "Okay, Ann, tell them what this means." Outside of class, however, I still had a reputation to keep, and Mr. Besse was still my enemy.

Memorial Day weekend I went camping in the wilds of Maine. No contact with the outside world. On Tuesday I came back to school and went straight to the cafeteria before first period to talk with my friends. Someone said, "Guess who died this weekend, Ann." In an Academy Award performance I dropped to my knees, clasped my hands together, and proclaimed to the heavens, "Please, Lord, let it be Mr. Besse!"

I heard a gasp and someone else mutter, "She doesn't know." I looked at the stunned faces around me and asked what was wrong. Someone quietly told me that in fact it *had* been Mr. Besse who, while tilling the earth for his garden, had suffered a fatal heart attack.

Another teacher finished his class, but I never went back. I have kept all the papers he ever passed out to us, and I still have all my graded work with his comments written on the tops of those pages. I can't part with them.

I cried writing this. He did so much for me and I couldn't even tell him. Mr. Besse was a brilliant man and as an adult I know he and I would have had a lot in common. I was so lucky to have had him in my life.

THE WAY TO TEACH

(It isn't so much
having a question to ask,
rather the ability
to create one)

and so
he let them have their games
until the tide was fully out
and when it was
he came upon the rocky beach
a maypole of a man
among the shouting children
and bending down
beside a magic pool
peering in
he waited

he waited
till a ring of faces gathered
at the edge of this attention
then slowly
reaching through the mirror
gave a sea anemone
a punch
who did

what sea anemones will do
quickly folding in
on what should have been a lunch

wow!

he said—eyes popping
then abruptly rising
but keeping in mind
the length of his legs
moved on up the beach
the children scrambling behind
with questions.

Ric Masten
poet, performer

JUDITH BELL UNGAR
attorney

—— w r i t i n g   a b o u t ——

PROFESSOR HOGAN
her college English teacher

A LONG ROW IN THE HOT SUN

His obituary in the *Illinois Quarterly* gave me a sad shock . . . and sparked memories. Professor Hogan was my English teacher for several courses at the University of Illinois. He had a great sense of humor, sometimes with an edge. His thoughts and gestures were large; he was eloquent without being pompous.

I see now I had a crush on him. I don't know if he knew it. I imagine coeds fell for him every year; we were his occupational hazard. He certainly never encouraged it by any inappropriate means. ("Could there be appropriate means?" he would ask at this point.) He was inherently a vital, warm, intelligent, appealing man, not his fault.

His creative writing course was marvelous. One day at the board he drew a shaggy cone. "Suppose you want to describe the view from the top of this mountain," he said. "You could just give the view from the peak: how small and faraway things below are, the thinness and coolness of the air. . . ." He tapped the peak with his chalk for emphasis.

"Or," he continued, lowering his arm, "you could start here instead." He made an *X* near the bottom of the mountain.

"Describe the base, the temperature, how far ahead you can see as you begin to climb. Then, when you—or your character—get halfway up"—another chalk mark—"stop and look around and give the scene from this vantage point: Feet hurt? Sweating? Walking slower? What do you see? Keep walking . . . stop there." This next *X* was three quarters of the way up. "Now what? Changes in vegetation? Tired? Exhilarated? Impatient? Those muscles in your calves weary? Thirsty? Tell us. Start walking again. Finally, the peak." He drew the last *X*.

"Now what do you see? Is your viewpoint richer because you achieved it in incremental stages? Because you changed your perspectives over time and space? Because you climbed up instead of starting at the top?"

Brilliant . . . he's brilliant, I thought.

The course culmination was a paper on the semester's topic: Manners and Morals. In the beginning I thought of manners as distant and weak cousins of morals. As we discussed situations in class, I reconsidered. By the end of the year I saw manners as outward manifestations of morals, significant in their own right. "You see the fork is dirty, and clean it with your napkin," Professor Hogan said. "Somebody at the next table sees you and gives you a dirty look. What bad manners, right? Really? Do you have bad manners for cleaning your fork or is the restaurant wrong for giving you a dirty fork?" Professor Hogan challenged us constantly. I worked hard in that class.

When the semester ended I gave my teachers postcards so they could send me my grades before the university issued the official reports. When the card from Professor Hogan arrived I read it over and over: "A long row in the hot sun." I had made an A on the final paper and in the course.

Like all great teachers, Professor Hogan taught more than the stated subject of the class. Now that I have climbed up to the 54-year mark on the mountain and done some teaching along the way, I know our class was an effort for him as well as for me. Living, like writing, is an incremental process of moving, building, slipping, climbing, reflecting. Professor Hogan pushed me in the right direction.

PEGGY LANDSMAN
poet, writer

—— w r i t i n g   a b o u t ——

MR. McCORMACK
her seventh-grade history teacher

When Mr. McCormack teaches about Paul Revere's ride, I can swear there's a horse in the room. I make sure to check the bottoms of my shoes before going to my next class. It is the 1962–63 school year. I am in Mr. McCormack's seventh-grade American History class at Millburn (New Jersey) Junior High School. Sandy-haired, blue-eyed, twenty-three-year-old Mr. McCormack looms above me, ancient and wise. He says he is five-foot-nine; he seems very tall. All of him is gorgeous. Mr. McCormack is the best teacher I've ever had; he is also the strictest, and at times the most unreasonable.

One day as he is letting us go, he suggests casually that we might find out something about the Tennessee Valley Authority. The next morning he asks for a volunteer to report on it. Not one hand is raised. McCormack is furious. He blows up. He bellows, "Now you all have an assignment! A twelve-page paper on the TVA. Due Monday." (Today is Friday.)

All weekend I debate: Do I bow down to this injustice—*his* injustice—or resist? A strange mixture of fear and misery impels me to the public library. I open up the *World Book Encyclopedia*. I take notes. At home I convert the notes into sentences and paragraphs. It's not nearly enough. I add details I remember from *Wild River*, the Montgomery Clift, Lee Remick movie about a woman who doesn't want to sell her home to the TVA. I come up with only nine pages, but my handwriting is small.

On Monday I turn in the paper. On Tuesday I get it back. A huge C– is written in red ink, clear across the first page. No one receives a higher grade. Our averages will be destroyed. We all agree: This is not fair. I say I'll speak to him.

At the end of the day I knock timidly on Mr. McCormack's door. In silvery tones he tells me to come in. "Can I talk with you about the TVA paper?" I ask. He says yes. "Everyone thinks it was unfair. You never said we *had* to do anything. And we don't think you should count the grade."

"I appreciate your coming to see me, but from now on when I make a suggestion, you'll know to follow it. And"—he wags a finger—"when you're told to write twelve pages, you should write twelve pages."

"But you said a paper should be like a bathing suit—brief enough to be interesting, long enough to cover the essentials."

"If your paper had been on the beach," he says, "it would have been arrested for indecent exposure." He falls silent for a moment. Gazes out the window. Then, locking his eyes to mine, he says, "I *do* respect you for your courage and straightforwardness." He unlocks. "See you tomorrow."

"See you tomorrow, *too,* Mr. McCormack!" I have failed in my mission, but I feel strangely elated.

Mr. McCormack sits at his desk adjusting the dial on the radio he has brought to class. We are listening to history in the making—the climax of the Cuban Missile Crisis. When the Russians turn their ships around, we cheer.

When Mr. McCormack teaches about the differences between individualism and collectivism, he begins by asking us questions. "How would you feel," he says, "if you got an A on a very important test, but everyone else failed?" Everyone gets excited. Everyone talks. Then he continues with that gleam in his eye, "Imagine *everyone* gets an A."

Mr. McCormack explains that it is wrong to ostracize someone for being a fairy, a homosexual. He tells us about Liberace— what a perfectly decent human being he is—and what hell he has been put through by some of the English press. When several students act out the limp wrist, he pounces. This is serious! It's all about individual liberty!

Mr. McCormack warns that anyone caught watching the clock or jumping up at the sound of the bell will be punished. We are to sit attentively until *he* dismisses us: If we're paying attention to the bell, we're not paying attention to him. Two of my class-mates ignore the warning. Bobby is assigned "Life Inside a Ping-Pong Ball." Jimmy receives "Why Most Meatballs Do Not Bounce." When they hand the papers in, Mr. McCormack makes quite a production out of ripping them up and tossing them into the wastebasket. Boy, are they mad! They mutter that they would give *anything* to get out of History! I would give anything to stay.

I long for The Day The Bell Never Rings. I want to sit for-ever—listening to and looking at dreamy Mr. McCormack. But the bell does me in. One morning, as I am lost in concentra-tion, paying attention *only* to what he is saying, it rings—and it startles me out of my socks. I jump. Mr. McCormack stops talking. He walks toward me, whistling. He seems almost glee-ful as he stands over me and announces: " 'The Similarities Between Me and Jack-in-the-Pulpit.' Two hundred and fifty words, not one word less. For tomorrow." It is useless to protest.

Before I hand over my paper, I plead with Mr. McCormack to read it. "It's funny," I tell him. "You'll love it!" He gives me one of his evil grins, tears it cleanly down the middle, and tosses it. But I don't let this bother me. I am positive that as soon as he is alone, he'll tape it back together and read it. It will inspire him. For his master's thesis, he will write "The Fruits of Creative Discipline."

Mr. McCormack goes to graduate school part-time now, at night. To fulfill the requirements and keep his job, he has to take "Toilet Training 101" and "Poster Making 102." He even has to do homework. As hard as I try, I just can't picture my Mr. McCormack as a student. And I can't stop wondering: What would it be like to be *his* teacher?

ROBERT REICH
Former Secretary, U.S. Department of Labor
— w r i t i n g a b o u t —

BILL JAVANE
his sixth-grade teacher

My best teacher? Mr. Bill Javane, sixth grade. He inspired me to think. He asked hard questions for which there were no correct answers, but which demanded an explanation of values, meaning, and culture. Mr. Javane taught me to love philosophy and great literature, which deal with these kinds of questions all the time. He forced me to create consistency out of seeming inconsistencies.

Valley Memories of Richard Dokey

I felt the surge of pride you feel at the success of someone you know, in this case my high school Creative Writing teacher. In the library at Sacramento State College I had found the short story "Sanchez" by Richard Dokey in a back issue of *The Southwest Review*. It had been more than a year since I'd been Dokey's student at Lincoln High School—a year that seemed, now that I was in college, to have taken place an eternity before. Yet Dokey's lessons remained vivid.

Dokey taught us to see as a writer sees—to look at life with an eye to capture the moment. He spoke to us of how he, as a writer, looked at skid row, Stockton, noted the facade of an old brick hotel, stopped to observe the way a Filipino fieldworker held his cigarette, or listened to how the spring rain sounded on a downtown street.

Richard Dokey saw Stockton with a poet's eyes and he imparted some of that poetry to us. He told us to write of our own experience. He taught us Hemingway and Steinbeck from a writer's point of view; because of Dokey, we saw authors as people, who created out of the same emotions we experienced.

I can still picture myself and my baseball teammate and childhood friend Tom Gulick, walking home on a March afternoon after Dokey's class. We lit cigarettes and smoked; we could smell the coming rain. We were not still boys and not yet men, though Tom would be married before he was twenty and his son is now older than we were then.

Instead of talking about baseball, Tom and I spoke about the writers we admired and the places they described. We spoke of Steinbeck's Salinas and Monterey, of Mark Twain's Mississippi River, of Hemingway's Michigan, of Kerouac's Lowell. We wanted to see the places we'd read about. We spoke of our childhood—now passing—and we felt the truth of what William Saroyan once called "the warm quiet valley of home." We walked between the Coast Range and The Sierra and we looked west to Mt. Diablo, the mountain that overlooked our youth. We wanted to leave the valley forever and never look back—and at the same time, to never leave Stockton, to never leave home.

We *felt* the poetry our teacher Richard Dokey never called poetry.

Dokey's writing is recognized. His story "Sanchez" has been anthologized a dozen times. Gary Soto, James Houston, and Gerald Haslam have all included his work with the best of California and West Coast writing. But what I best remember and appreciate are Dokey's qualities as a teacher. He did for us what I try to do for my writing students now: help them slow down, observe, and trust their best instincts, and so catch the beauty, poignancy, and poetry of themselves, alive upon an earth moving so quickly through time.

THE TEACHER

For Robert Detweiler

If laughter's the brightest flower on the
Lord's lawn He grafted on you His green thumb:
when lines furrow by your eyes we see jokes
building like spring rain and your delight in
them doubles our fun

What do we want from our friends if not a
lifting once in a while of the world's weight?
I see you hunched at your desk eyes inches
from a book light beams slanted with dust mim-
icking galaxies:

motes of gold with their satellites circling
the sun Beauty's everywhere miracles
daily and something lit the world like a
wick: you were glad to call it God What we
need's not judgment but

love you'd tell us which doesn't mean that Dean
So & so isn't full of shit Around
the country now students at their daily
tasks stop every once in a while and smile
at some memory

of you slouched by the board turning toward them
to ask *OK who watched 'Star Trek' last night?*
beginning the dialogue: remembering
not only how you were funny but how
you made them realize

Though the big things happen outside of books
books too are vital: our best words and thoughts
pooling on paper oases in a
desert of dying verbs granting our parched
selves this rare chance: Drink

Peter Meinke
writer, retired professor

CURTIS SLIWA
Founder, Guardian Angels

—— w r i t i n g a b o u t ——

ALLAN TOPEL
his fifth-grade teacher

 When I walked into Mr. Topel's classroom that first day, I
was convinced a terrible mistake had been made transferring me to a new school. The room was cluttered with easels
and, preparing to do artwork, students wore smocks. *Ain't for
me,* I thought and just knew this would be one short experiment.

The next day, however, Mr. Topel passed out copies of the *New York Times* and we read about what was happening out in the world. For someone who hadn't read anything but *Weekly Reader* in school, the *Times* was pretty exciting.

Though Mr. Topel brought passion to every subject, I liked current events best. He created a dynamic atmosphere in which everyone wanted to soak up information and ideas, and then share them with the class. Never before or since has anyone stoked that kind of fire in my mind: I wanted to devour information so much I read every word on the cereal box each morning.

Everyone felt this excitement. Mr. Topel fueled an intellectual competition, and no one wanted to be left behind. Usually kids came up with all sorts of excuses to get out of class—you know, triple whiplash and herniated uvulas—or guys put their mouths on the radiator and then yelled to go to the nurse, just to skip class. But in Mr. Topel's class, we *wanted* to be there. We didn't want to miss one day.

We'd work all week; we were into it mind, body, and soul. Class would crescendo on Friday when we would engage in debates: Johnson versus Goldwater, things like that. We wanted to come in strong for him, for our classmates, and for ourselves.

In our debates we couldn't just spew rhetoric or we'd be annihilated. We had to take positions on these urgent issues, and back those positions with evidence. I learned to speak to anyone and to take on all challengers using the powerful weapon of information. This skill has served me for over thirty years.

The passion for learning has also stayed with me to this day, and I thank Allan Topel for instilling it. He developed my curiosity and desire to know everything I could. And he taught me to use this knowledge effectively. Allan Topel taught me to have confidence in myself, to communicate my thoughts to anyone, and to back up what I said with factual evidence. I've fought many verbal battles over the last decade, and the foundation Mr. Topel gave me has helped me persevere through them all.

Mr. Topel is now a principal and I've been fortunate to see him again and thank him for changing my life.

CHLOE LeMAY
retired teacher, writer

—— w r i t i n g   a b o u t ——

PAULINE BRUMMIT
her elementary school teacher

I still get hungry when I hear "Onward Christian Soldiers"; we sang it when we marched to lunch in third grade. In fact we sang all day in third grade. We sang "Good Morning, Miss Pauline" to the teacher, we sang the alphabet, we chanted multiplication tables, and at recess, we played singing games. "Go in and out the window . . . go forth and face your lover" still reverberate in my mind.

I lived on a farm with my parents and grandparents three miles from a small mountain town. My elders were determined that I would *not* go to the nearby one-room school. Grandpa, retired with not much else to do, taught me to read so early I can't remember not reading. Mama taught me arithmetic and how to use real money.

One August, the State said I had to go to school, so Grandpa took me to Duffield Academy in town. He told them I should start in fifth grade. The principal looked skeptical. He handed me a newspaper and told me to read the main story, which I did, pronouncing all the words correctly. Then he said, "Does she have any idea what it means?"

"Ask her," said Grandpa. I proceeded to explain about President Harding and the Teapot Dome Scandal (mostly quoting Grandpa, of course). The principal sighed. Then he led us to the empty fifth-grade classroom. When I sat down, I couldn't see over the top of the desk. We tried fourth grade with the same result. Finally in the third-grade classroom, my nose was above the desktop; it was agreed that was where I would start in September. Grandpa paid the tuition required of county children going to a city school.

That's how the best thing to happen to me in this life came about: Miss Pauline Brummit became my first teacher. We third graders thought she was as beautiful as any fairy princess she read to us about.

Miss Brummit said history was made by people and we were going to learn about people. Davy Crockett had lived here, Daniel Boone had passed through there and killed a bear, Sam Houston came from just over the mountain. Andrew Jackson held the first court west of the Alleghenies under a tree still living by the bridge. Abraham Lincoln was brought here to visit relatives when he was a child. One day, she measured on the wall how tall Lincoln was when he was president, then had Tommy come stand under it. "See?" she said. "That's only twelve inches taller than you. Who knows, you may grow to be as tall as Lincoln." Tommy grinned and swaggered to his seat. She awakened us to a proud heritage, gave us what today would be called self-esteem.

In Junior High, I learned to hate history. We had to keep notebooks with outlines of events and memorize dates. It was dreary and devoid of human interest.

When I got to high school, to my delight Miss Brummit was there teaching history. We learned about ancient lands; she read the poetry of Homer to us, and had us memorize some. She made dead Romans come alive.

As Seniors, we had her for the detested American History. But we were heartened to learn General Lafayette had not been much older than we were. We were fascinated when Dolly Madison saved the original Constitution and a portrait of George Washington, as she fled the White House in a wagon, leaving her dinner for the British soldiers to eat. We were hooked.

Miss Brummit laughed at the notebooks the Supervisors wanted. But they must have threatened her, for one weekend in spring she had us throwing together a semblance of an outline and putting it into a notebook. After high school came World War II, which scattered everyone.

I heard Miss Brummit had become one of the State Supervisors. Home on vacation, I ran into her. She grabbed me by the shoulders and said I had to teach. "You always liked history," she said. "I need history teachers."

I told her I was married, had to leave, and couldn't do that right now. She seemed to think that was no excuse. Later I did teach and tried to model my methods on hers. Like her, I stayed in trouble with my supervisors who still wanted children to learn by rote. In fact I struggled to model my whole life on her philosophy: Look for the good in everything; bring out the best in others; never say can't, never stop learning.

I went to see her years later. She was sick, lying on the sofa, but brightened up when I arrived. She got out pictures of my old third grade. I told her I still woke up worrying about Chinese children who might fall off the earth after she told us it was round. She laughed and said today the earth was pear-shaped and the Chinese would go into orbit. I told her how much she had meant to me, and she said I was one of her favorite pupils. I'm sure she meant it—and said it to all her students.

CHAPTER 3

THE SAGE

About those who helped students discover important truths about the world and themselves

Education's purpose is to replace an empty mind with an open one.

—*Malcolm S. Forbes*

Middle Spirits

Written for the first female professor at
California State University, Long Beach—
Dr. Virginia Ringer, who taught philosophy

The ones who knew you stand
ankle on ankle
around the cherry blossoms,
near your classical air.

To warm marble.
To trace sculpture marks,
to find arms strong unbreakable,
to meet prominent eyes
which did not lose
out to a bony skull,
we stand here, in mourning.

We would have wished
better for you, our lady
soul. A stronger finish
for a strong woman.

Instead, we remember how
in class we watched you,
every semester, tell the story
of the prisoners

while you marked
on the blackboard with a paltry
bit of yellow chalk. You told of three
World War II prisoners

confined to cells of lapis excilis,
the stones of no worth.
Darkness, save for
a slot of yellow light
seen through the underbelly

of the door. The first was an athlete
in his twenties. For days
his eyes dampened the gravel floor.
And when his tears were gone,
he dried up: an angel in perfect form.

The second, a middle-aged man,
sure of his demons,
tried to crawl to the way out,
by scraping for the tunnel
he knew, like air, must exist.

The skin peeled back
from his nails, and he applauded
hollow sounds until the food
sent under the door was too brittle
for him to swallow.

The third, you said, was a woman
well into her eighties,
a philosopher at the Sorbonne.
She sat in a solitary cell
until her eyes grew accustomed
to the new darkness: A teleological fish
being hatched.

For two long years she scrawled
on the walls mapping continents,
diagramming poetry, working through old
long-forgotten logic problems.
All that she could remember.

"I'll survive on my knowledge,"
she said to no one.
The sharp point of her contraband
pencil shining in the shadows.

And when the officials opened the
cell door after the war, she had
to be fitted with special goggles
because the sun was too severe
for her to bear.

Today, your students are sure
that you exist. Strong somewhere.
Between the men and the angels,

on a cold stone wall, we see you
scratching out the formulas of Lucretius,
reciting the attributes of atoms;
we see you building cities in our souls.

Millicent C. Borges
technical writer, college instructor

MELISSA JUELLIS
college student

—— writing about ——

MICHAEL WAYMAN
her tennis coach

I used to hate the game of tennis. There wasn't any sense of purpose behind it; I only played for my father, so I had no desire to practice or to improve. Then one day I met Michael Wayman and from that day forward, my life was different—and better.

To become one of Michael's students, you had to try out for his tennis class. Rumors streamed through the tennis club about his students: how hard he made them work and how good they were. I couldn't understand why people would want to run so much and train so hard, or why anyone would want to play tennis for four hours at a time.

Yet my curiosity lured me to try out. I remember that first day on his team clearly: As I walked in, I could hear Michael lecturing about tennis strategies in his wonderful British accent. When we practiced, I recall how tired I got from running and running, and drilling and drilling, and more running and more drilling. But beyond the exhaustion, I vividly remember his students: They listened to him; they hung on every word, every comment.

I didn't notice it then, but in retrospect I get shivers: His students all had the same look in their eyes that spoke of a passion for the game, a love for every moment in pursuit of both personal and team excellence. All his students seemed to move together and play with the same rhythm. I looked around at everyone as we did yet another 100 gut crunches and, as I moaned, I saw a smile on the face of each teammate. I too came to hang on his words and to smile through the pain as he called for 100 more sprints.

Michael didn't compliment us unless we deserved it, so when he did, it meant even more. Something about him told me he cared and wanted me to improve. With that concern, I was able to push myself to the limit. I believed him when he reminded us that every point we won was a reflection of how hard we worked.

Once he said something I'll never forget: "You can't just sit there complaining about how good your opponent is. You've got to ask yourself, 'Since she *is* that good, what do I need to do to beat her?'" These are words I've carried with me and applied to other realms of my life. Learning how to work hard and believe in my tennis success led to greater personal expectations in all that I do. Michael couldn't tolerate slackers and neither can I.

Were I to see him tomorrow, I'd thank Michael Wayman for giving me a passion for tennis and for life. But, hey, talk is cheap—let's play.

CORA

Cora was my second-grade teacher. She taught
me how to read in a white trailer-turned-classroom
that sat among many. Two columns of remodeled
mobile homes connected by city pavement—
my elementary school

Every day she talked of sounds associated with letters
Long a, short u, diphthong, the upside down e
Sounds, words, nouns, verbs, phrases, sentences
melodious

Cora taught me Negro spirituals
I sang, clapped and wandered
cotton field and mansions not our own
tenacious Congo meter
In that great gettin' up morning
poetry

Cora sits in the corner of a white room
death grew on her brain—they removed it.
Her shaven head and empty eyes
tell me they removed more than death

She does not remember the mobile homes
the spirituals

she does not remember me
I read the absence of Cora

I kiss the white beanie cap on Cora's head
I close the door as she pats her feet to forgotten rhythms
In that great gettin' up morning
Fare-ye-well

Roberta Young-Jackson

THE REVEREND CHRISTOPHER BOWHAY
Episcopalian priest
—— writing about ——
THE REVEREND RICHARD GILMAN
Episcopalian priest

When I got the phone call telling me Dixie had died, I found, as with so many other circumstances, it was something for which he had prepared me.

"Grief is mysterious," he had said four years earlier, as we roared across the Richmond bridge to the weekly Mass he offered for a tiny but faithful mission in Marin County. I drove him as part of my seminary duties. "It is something modern science cannot understand. Doctors have taken countless tests on those who are grieving: blood tests, brain scans, X-rays, and the like. But they find no discernible physiological changes or measurable manifestations of grief. Everything in the body is exactly as it was before the loss. But," he added, tapping his chest, "there is a hurt, an ache one feels as strongly as any bruise or cut. It is something only the poets can explore or talk about."

The Reverend Richard H. Gilman III ("Dixie" to his friends) was no poet. He was an engineer, trained in the Marine Corps in World War II and afterwards at Cal Tech. An avowed "right-brainer," he was most comfortable in the world of straight lines and details. Abstract symbols, the building blocks of poetry, simply eluded him. (He once told me about getting hopelessly lost in an airport looking for the bathroom. "Why can't they just put up a sign saying 'Men' and 'Women' anymore? Since when has a man looked like two vertical lines and a woman looked like a goddamned triangle?")

While he was no poet, he was acquainted with grief. In the course of his life and travels around the world he had lost two wives and two children, infant twins who died in his arms at the hospital. And yet in the ten years I knew him I never heard him bewail the tragedies of his life. He seemed emotionally incapable of wallowing in melodramatic self-pity or self-absorption, even though my experiences with the human heart in the Confessional show that such incapability is never effortless.

F. Scott Fitzgerald once wrote, "There are no Second Acts in American lives." Too many Americans believe by the time they reach their sixties they have already achieved all they are going to achieve, and their one-act play of life is coming to a close. They begin to wait to clear the stage. But when Father Gilman was sixty-five, after retiring from building dams and bridges across the world in his own successful engineering firm, he decided to go to seminary and offer to serve as a priest in a then-tiny, fragile diocese of traditional Episcopalians. He was working in the Berkeley office of that diocese (on which he had an immeasurable impact and for which he never took a salary) when I met him.

I was a confused, semi-barbaric English major. At first I was charmed by his apparently gruff exterior, a tough old Marine with a salty view of life, haloed by smoke from his ever-present unfiltered cigarettes. Here was no plastic saint demonstrating a phony piety. But later I became enamored by his more essential interior, his style of almost habitual, unself-conscious self-sacrifice. It seemed there was never anything he wouldn't do to help someone. And when he helped, he had a way of thanking them afterwards, as if *they* had done *him* a favor by giving him a chance to assist. In the fusion of these two styles he proved to be a true priest, a person who conveys the grace of God by personalizing it, communicating God while remaining himself.

Some people think faith in God is a feeling, an emotion, a comforting sentiment, a druggy buzz into which one escapes to avoid reality. But Father Gilman advocated and demonstrated that Christians are supposed to be reality-oriented. We aren't supposed to escape life with its occasional sorrows and sufferings. We want to confront it, work with it, think about it, and deal with it. Our means of dealing with life is to love through and beyond personal tragedy. Faith, *fides,* means loyalty, duty. Faith is the quality of a soldier, and Father Gilman remained a faithful soldier for the love of God until his life's end. His reality-oriented approach to life and God reassured me I too could find sanity and love in the priesthood, and through priesthood I might be able to help others find these things.

If teaching is merely a transmission of data through discourse and tests, Father Gilman was never officially my teacher. But since teaching, in its highest expression, is an inculcation of and an inspiration to a more noble attitude and outlook on life, he was one of the most profound teachers I have ever known. He taught me that the joy of the saints is never achieved in one moment, but in a lifetime of loves and sufferings, surrendering to God by giving oneself to others, and a daily oblation of small sacrifices of self.

Toward the end of his life he found a new beginning that incorporated all the events that had forged his life and transfigured them with greater meaning. This meaning, which is the quest for God and the desire to love on every level of one's being, survives and transcends all tragedies and losses, including death. And so, after I received the call telling me Dixie had died, even though I began to weep as I had never wept before, I remembered that, just as the tears he had shed occasionally had ultimately been transformed into joy, my current sorrow would one day be transformed into a greater love, whose vision Dixie first taught me to look for and which Dixie now sees in His fullness.

The night before Father Gilman died, my bishop, who was also close to him, had a dream. Dixie came into his bedroom and stood before him, crying. At first the bishop thought Dixie was crying because he was so sorry to go, to leave his friends behind. But then he remembered Dixie often wept when he saw or heard something beautiful: a magnificent hymn, children in a new church, an act of kindness. And then the bishop realized Dixie was crying because he was seeing Something beautiful even as he was dying. Moved by that vision, the bishop placed a special plaque above the bench upon which Dixie sat in the chapel where he prayed every evening. It is a quote from the Revelation of St. John that reads:

> *They shall hunger no more, neither thirst any more; neither shall the sun light on them, or any heat. For the Lamb which is in the midst of the throne shall feed them, and shall lead them into living fountains of waters: and God shall wipe away all tears from their eyes.*
>
> *(Rev. VII:16–17)*

YELLOW

still, death-dirtied now, the daffodils—
dozen once, eleven in the vase upon my sill—
await disposal. But, oh the sight
last week! Just a week?

At the first, bordered round the patch
we dignify as garden—out past the redwood deck,
circling the half-keg containered lemon tree,
flowers color-matching fruit—some few lemons

heavy on the overhanging limbs—some few
bulb-promised, now erupted
daffodils.

Miss Bristol, dry as barren branch,
my nature teacher in The Bronx,
could you know? Is there any way
that I could reach beyond your grave—
probable since I, now in my sixth decade,
remember you wizened, wise and old—
Are there accolades that I may offer you,
some show of gratitude, acknowledgement?

In that grey room so long ago,
trees greened from words you spoke
into the city-dark. Small woodland creatures
bounded through that class,
never seen along macadam, guttered streets
where such trees as were, small cramped roots
protected under iron grilles, never hosted squirrels
nor shaded sylvan-gladed animals—ring-eyed raccoons,
red flash of fox, turkey vulture on a Texas road—
all seen close to, so many years removed
from your P.S. 90 room—chalk dust the soil
from which we grew a consciousness, a love, a hunger,
for the woodsy world beyond our city parks,
for sights of life beyond our city streets,
for daffodils . . .

Miss Bristol, did you ever know
the rock garden that we planned—
a simulant within a cardboard box—
the garden that we never grew
yet took root and spread?

Miss Bristol, could you have guessed
the thread from me to you? And even now,
as I discard the withered yesterday,
looking back, remembering you, I look forward to
next year's daffodils.

Pearl Stein Selinsky
retired teacher, poet

ADRIENNE EISEN GREENHEART

—— w r i t i n g a b o u t ——

MRS. ZAK

her Hebrew school teacher

NEVER FORGET

Mrs. Zak is my Hebrew school teacher. Mrs. Zak is saying, "A *v* with a dot inside is a *b*." No one is listening. Barry Rosenthal raises his hand and says we can't concentrate today because last night the Brady Bunch got stuck in Hawaii, and we need to leave class early so we don't miss the beginning of tonight's episode.

We are all embarrassed for Barry's bad behavior. But we are quietly waiting for Mrs. Zak's answer.

Mrs. Zak is quietly waiting too. She is looking at us.

She tells us to close our books and she passes out licorice to the class. This is a big deal because you can't make the guttural sounds with food in your mouth.

Then she tells us she was at Auschwitz. She says she will tell us a story about it. She folds her hands on top of her desk, and she tells us from the beginning, from the time when she was a fifth grader, like us. She tells us her mother didn't let go of her hand for three days. But they were separated anyway, and Mrs. Zak never saw her mother again. I think about if I never saw my mother again, and I can't believe Mrs. Zak isn't crying. Her hands are shaking though.

She says if you don't tell stories, people can pretend it never happened. I think that even though she yells at us for not doing our homework, she likes us because she is letting us see her shake. I want to do something nice for Mrs. Zak, like do my homework every week. But I know I can't do that, so I decide to be a person who holds stories.

She lets us touch her tattoo, and it is black and bumpy.

She lets us out of class early.

THE POCKETKNIFE

So unexpectedly, last night, I remembered him:
    Antonio, at the volunteer fire meeting,
    unwrapping the new pike,
    needed something to rip
    through the strapping tape.

"Here," I said, and tossed him my pocketknife:
    there in mid-air,
    between my throwing hand
    and Antonio's open palm,
    the brass studded knife
    turned slow-motion,
    lighting in my heart
    bald and black-suited,
    skinny, shiny Mr. Schenck.

When I was a kid in his Sunday School class,
he was so old, so old he had always been old,
so old he had been born old,
so old he knew everything,
without fuss or passion,
quietly knowing everything
there was to know,
or think about,
or love.

And then off he went, one wet Pennsylvania winter,
to Florida. Florida! Paradise, Eden!
All that sun, ocean, sand, shells, and skin.
The Sunday he returned, spring's first teasing touch
returned as well. My damp socks were still chill,
but the light warm on my capless head.
Mr. Schenck had a little gift for me;
from his thin hands I shyly took and cupped
a slim box, tissued and ribboned.

When I opened it there at the many-boyed,
hand-nicked Sunday School table,
into my fingers fell my first knife:
folding, pearl-handled,
a palm tree, the sea,
Miami Beach.
Ah, Mr. Schenck not only knew
everything there was to know;
he sensed the way a boy could fly,
and how a boy could sit so still,
with hints that a whole wide world
can be in his pocket,
and that's gonna be OK, always.

W. A. Ewing
publisher, poet, author

ALEX CAMPBELL
writer, teacher, attorney

—— w r i t i n g a b o u t ——

MRS. WEEKS
her daughter's kindergarten teacher

It all started in childhood. Not mine, my daughter's. Polly's kindergarten teacher was the best one she ever had. My daughter may disagree, since later a few outstanding educators crossed her path, but in my opinion Mrs. Weeks was the crown jewel.

She'd been trained by example and scholarship at British infant schools. In these classrooms kids were encouraged to be kids but to interact imaginatively among the downsized trappings of an adult world. They role-played the jobs of police and firefighters, busily shared chores in a housekeeping corner, shopped in a pretend store with paper money, built shelters with large blocks, and listened to stories from cultures on the other side of the world.

No coloring books could be found in Mrs. Weeks' classroom. Art projects resulted in eighteen completely different masterpieces rather than eighteen renditions of her example. The theory was that if Madame Curie hadn't been encouraged to color outside the lines, science would have been set back a generation or two.

There was a waiting list for Mrs. Weeks' class; I used all my clout and the clout of some mere acquaintances to get Polly in. When we went for a preview visit before school began, my daughter explored the classroom while Mrs. Weeks and I chatted. The object in the room that most intrigued Polly was an octopus preserved in a large jar of formaldehyde. My daughter recognized it from her picture book of sea animals, but since it was slightly discolored, she asked, just to make sure. "Is this an octopus?"

"Yes," said Mrs. Weeks. "It used to be alive, but after it died, we put it in that jar so we could look closely at the suction cups on its legs."

"It has eight legs," Polly said. I beamed.

The teacher and I wandered out to the playground so I could see what it had to offer my active daughter. Before we knew it, several minutes had passed and Polly had not joined us. I called back to her. In her own time, she came out through the open classroom door, carrying the heavy jar full of octopus. Just as she crossed the threshold, it slipped out of her chubby hands and fell to the blacktop, smashing to pieces. The octopus without its liquid environment was a gray, limp rag; formaldehyde began to stain the playground surface with its thick, slippery ooze. Worst of all, the chemical's deathly smell began to waft back into the classroom on the late summer breeze.

Polly looked horrified. I glanced at Mrs. Weeks with an apology on my lips. She, however, a veteran of accidental pees and vomits on new shoes, was cheerfully reassuring. Without hesitation, she exclaimed, "Oh my! Good thing it was already dead!"

"How can we replace it?" I asked.

"The ocean's full of them," she said. "Not to worry. Let's get this glass cleaned up." We steered Polly back inside where she quickly became occupied by the garments in the dress-up trunk. In a few minutes a custodian arrived with a bucket and mop. He grinned at Mrs. Weeks as if she were his ticket to job security.

It wasn't long before the first parent-teacher conference; I went to learn how Polly was doing. I already knew how Mrs. Weeks was doing because Polly told me almost every day: "Mrs. Weeks scolded Frankie today. He pushed Lucy off the climbing bars. Mrs. Weeks says that's not how you tell someone you want a turn." Or "Sammy cried a long time when his grandma dropped him off and Mrs. Weeks said it was not a good day for Sammy and we should be extra nice to him."

I went to the conference for Mrs. Weeks' point of view and to hear the stories about Polly. She started out positively; teachers learn to do that in college. Being parents is full of enough surprises, they should be spared severe shock at a teacher conference. Even the most incorrigible child's parents are told something good at first.

"She can identify fifteen types of whales by name and classify each as baleen or toothed," Mrs. Weeks began. I puffed up with pride. "But," she said, leaning toward me from across the small table, "the other day she brought me the toy iron from the housekeeping corner and asked me what it is." I glanced over at the pint-size ironing board and saw that the facsimile resting on it was an accurate one, ruling out the obvious excuse. This left only the real reason; I was compelled to reveal a family secret. "Mrs. Weeks, we don't do much ironing at our house." I checked the crease in my best slacks; it was quickly losing whatever peak it had once had. Now I faced a professional's diagnosis that my daughter was domestically challenged.

Mrs. Weeks' voice promptly brought me back to reality. "Well, there's not much future in it, I guess—unless you plan to be a laundry mogul." She had the gift of putting anything in perspective.

I changed the subject by asking a question suggested in one of those magazines displayed at the supermarket checkout counter: "What is her reading level?"

"She can read the things that are important to her, like 'toilet,' 'caution,' and 'whale.' That's just where she should be for now. And she has plenty of good friends."

If Mrs. Weeks were alive today, I would tell her Polly not only reads lots more English words, but she speaks and reads Japanese. And she graduated magna cum laude from an Ivy League college. Those friends she made in kindergarten? An actor, a farmer, a legislator, and a TV personality, they live in Chicago, Washington, D.C., Michigan, New Zealand, and Japan.

The world they heard stories about has become smaller, allowing them to get together every year or so. And when they do, it is as if the years melt away and they are back in the sandbox—taking turns and knowing when each other needs a little extra kindness.

THE WAY IT WAS

Christmas at Marshall Field's
Mother chose a dozen ladies' handkerchieves,
linen squares of varying degrees of fanciness,
depending on how much the intended recipient
admired President Roosevelt. The saleslady
wrapped each in white tissue paper
and placed it in a shiny white folder sealed
with a gold sunburst.

At home I made a card for each; cut stars
from tinfoil, white snowdrifts, brown deer
and green triangle-trees of construction paper,
and pasted them on a midnight blue ground.

The ritual of the hankies was also celebrated
at Easter, but while the Easter hankie
might be sprigged with satin-stitch buttercups
and lilies-of-the-valley, hints of green
and daffodil, the Christmas hankie,
however heavily embroidered or lace-encrusted
and appliquéd, was always white.
Pure, Mother said, as the driven snow.
I have always puzzled at my mother's
odd determination to deal with the products

of my teachers' noses, but these tokens
were indeed for them.

Miss Collins returned from World War II
a commander in the WAVES, awesome
in uniform, white hat chic with braid
and bright brass ropes and anchors.
The school's corridors hove to for her.
Fine she wished to teach us math again,
but what was our principal to do
when she announced her coming marriage?
A teacher might, perhaps, if not virgin,
be long widowed, or have been deserted,
then divorced discreetly; but Mr. Blair
could not order a war heroine
better to burn than to marry.
She was a head taller than he and now
a trained killer. It wasn't long until
The Biannual Handkerchief for Teacher
had gone a-glimmering. Previously
they had been expected to cry a lot.

Alice Wirth Gray
writer

SHEL STEINBERG
Intercultural Management Services

—— w r i t i n g a b o u t ——

THOMAS HOPKINS
his education professor

When I enrolled in "Theory of Curriculum Development," I thought it would be one of those boring nuts-and-bolts college courses on how to write lesson plans. To my surprise Thomas Hopkins never discussed them.

Hopkins believed all learning starts with need; our first assignment was to write a short description of a need we hadn't yet resolved. I handed in a trite statement about needing to learn how to write better lesson plans. After the next class Hopkins asked to see a few of us after class. He bluntly told us our need statements were way off target. He said he wanted us to write about a *real* need we had as individuals—not some mechanical statement of a low-level need.

I decided to test him and wrote about a need for my wife and I to decide whether to return to practicing Judaism so our son, Gary, would have this religious base of ethics and morals as he grew up. During the following class, Hopkins asked me to see him afterwards. When we talked, he told me I was beginning to understand what he was talking about with regard to need. He invited me to lunch at the faculty club the following week.

We met and he asked me to talk about how my wife and I had

come to identify this need. I talked steadily for over an hour, spurred by just a few questions from Hopkins. Toward the end of our lunch meeting I had pretty much resolved the issue.

Hopkins asked if I thought I had come to any conclusion. I told him I thought I had. He asked me if I understood the process I had gone through to arrive at the solution. I said I did. Then Hopkins told me I had an A for the course; he couldn't teach me any more than that. He also said I didn't have to come to class anymore if I didn't want to. I didn't miss one.

Hopkins showed me that unless you address needs that students have and involve them in the learning process, the learning that takes place tends to be technical and mechanistic. This perspective, which I would take with me into graduate work in education, was a valuable gift from a visionary professor.

SEAMSTRESS

For Hazel Shelton

Hazel was a seamstress with a feel for fabric
and the way things fit, with a flare for mischief
and what to wear for the next adventure.
She taught me sewing for 4-H and
Make-It-with-Wool. In those years
when I thought ineptitude had been invented
to accommodate my mother, I could escape

to Hazel's sewing porch where colored
threads scriggled like hieroglyphs on the
carpet and arms of chairs, and you didn't
dare walk barefoot for the pins. She had come
north with a reliable Singer machine that
she'd never replace, and the light, always ablaze
above her work table, was an open invitation
to the gaiety of a flapper's delta. What did I know
of southern belles? Had she lived like Zelda, or
Tennessee Williams women? Though I'm foggy
on details, stories sped with fast cars, rash
decisions, breathy laughter trailing behind like
Isadora's scarves. As I cross-stitched hems and
sewed bound buttonholes, Louisiana of the thirties
jazzed itself into the room with all its risk and
chanciness, single-minded horns blowing vast holes in
sweltering gardenia-scented nights, gowns
cut on the bias and clinging across protruding
pelvic bones, see-through chiffon and satin that
absorbed the light, and the oil man who danced
her through it all, then swept her away out West.

Sam was an imposing figure of a man,
tall as an oil derrick, now white-haired and
still good looking, but sad as a zoo animal,
his territory reduced to the four-block radius
between his recliner and the bars. He'd greet
me with the charm of a southern gentleman,

then retreat beyond the range of the feminine.
But Hazel and I had good times
around tailoring tutorials, facing interfacing.
I learned to hide the knot and bury the loose ends,
to adapt the pattern to fit exactly, means
of adjusting—gussets, pleats and darts,
ways of making things hold to your dreams,
like basting, bias binding and reinforced seams.
My waist was thin as a fairy princess
when she fitted me for the prom
in a bodice so tight as to assure I'd be all night
breathless. She knew secrets about design,
fitting into and realigning. I felt she could have
dressed me to be at ease on Jay Gatsby's verandah.
Nothing like that ever happened in Wyoming,
but she made me blossom like magnolias
in our high school gym and become the
princess bride in our charmless brick church
built in the fifties to get us through.
There wasn't much Hazel couldn't do
except, though she withered trying,
mend the seams of a man who retired young
with nothing to do with his hands.

                    Maureen Tolman Flannery

CHAPTER 4

THE MAESTRO

*About those who helped students
express themselves in the arts*

My heart is singing for the joy of this morning. A
miracle has happened! The light of understanding
has shone upon my little pupil's mind, and behold,
all things are changed!

—*Annie Sullivan*

SQUARE DANCING WITH SISTER ROBERT CLAIRE

I.

First week of junior high, Kel wised off to her
same as he'd done to the one all year before.
I can still see it. Her so short, the uppercut put
all her weight under it. The whack of her pudgy fist
against the V of his chin. Kel arching a back-dive, landing
legs up, desks dominoing halfway up the row.
Sweet Jesus, she was tough, but bless her the first one
who liked boys best and didn't carry grudges.

II.

But she sure as hell wasn't one of the almost-pretty nuns
you could almost imagine out there in the world.
Picture pie-faced Lou from Abbott and Costello,
lumpy-looking in any duds but now add a thick black
floor-length habit with dozens of folds, hidden pockets.
Around her waist rosary beads big as marbles
dangling to where her knees would be.
Hair, ears, and neck under a stiff wimple,
she roamed the aisles like a chubby penguin.

III.

One week she dragged us into the gym
and the alien world of square dancing—and girls.

Shedding blazers, ties, and shoes, we were cornered.
In sweat socks and knee socks, we shuffled like prisoners,
allemande left and *do-si-do* stranger than *Dominus vobiscum.*
Robert Claire stood on a chair trying to clap rhythm
into our dumb feet, sometimes leaping down, landing
light as a blackbird. She'd skip and twirl among us
arm over arm until her habit billowed like a gown,
face glowing, urging her stumblebums toward lessons
of possibility and romance she brought from a life before.
Reluctantly, we learned, began to move together, touch, let go,
God's clumsy children graceful under her familiar hand.

Michael Cleary
college professor

PATRICIA TYLER
loan processor, artist, photographer
—— w r i t i n g a b o u t ——
MRS. CAMPBELL
her grammar school music teacher

GIFT FOR A WARRIOR MUSICIAN

My mother came from a long line of amateur and
professional musicians. The line, however, ended with
me. But Mama, Irish and undaunted, remained in denial
about that fact throughout her life. She equated my lack of

innate musical talent in particular with a lack of normally functioning brain cells in general. One country teacher disagreed.

I will always remember Mrs. Campbell, my grammar school music teacher. Not because she was a whizbang at music. And certainly not because she inspired me to become a world renowned musician. But she inspired me nonetheless.

Even my mother became impressed with this extraordinarily tall, buxom country woman. Mrs. Campbell's salt-and-pepper hair was pulled back in a bun. Her oversized torso was usually adorned in muted gingham. She was held upright by sensible black oxfords with square two-inch heels. Yet even my mother, city born and bred, the most beautiful and petite of all the forties fashion queens, grew to appreciate Mrs. Campbell.

By the end of my third musically unsuccessful year in our tiny rural grammar school, Mama, in desperation, rushed me off to discuss Mrs. Campbell's *after*-school fourth-grade music class. "Helen," she greeted my prospective extracurricular miracle worker, "can you see what you can do with her?" Mama often spoke to other grown-ups as if I were not in the room. She usually persuaded them to do her bidding too. I stood like a statue overhearing her suggestions that I start out with piano, since she had recently inherited one. I had the feeling Mama was up to her old tricks again. And I was right. The next day my lessons began.

Plunk! Plunk! "OOPS!" Plunk! Plunk! "OOPS!" I hated the sound of my plunks. And I was humiliated by each "OOPS" that compulsively popped from my mouth following each errant plunk. I fantasized that if I could just stop "oops"ing, my horrible plunks would be less noticeable. After months of my plunks-

and-oops routine Mama conceded that perhaps I was not a born pianist. But it didn't end there. I knew it wouldn't.

When Solomon Berstien moved away to Eureka, Mama suggested I utilize the clarinet he'd left behind. His clarinet and I were occasionally able to emit small gasps, but after months of clarinet practice, not one full melodious distinguishable note ever passed from Solomon's clarinet. Mrs. Campbell suggested to Mama that perhaps I didn't have the lungs for a wind instrument. Mama, however, would concede nothing so early in the game.

At about that time Shirley Fostermeyer, third violinist in the sixth-grade quartet, died an untimely death. When just enough time had passed to be barely appropriate, Mama asked Mrs. Campbell, "How do you think she'd do on the violin, Helen?" Mrs. Campbell's knees buckled. Then she pulled herself together and gazed down at my mother.

"I suppose we could try. But first consider this: Maybe her innate talent does not lie in music. Perhaps—" But Mama abruptly interrupted her. "Oh, she's musical all right. Music runs in the family. It's just a matter of finding the right instrument. And I so much want her to take part in the school recital next year. Her grandmother would adore it."

Mrs. Campbell reluctantly passed me Shirley's violin. *My* knees buckled. Accepting the battered violin case and its precious contents, I felt tears well in my eyes as I scrutinized my saddle oxfords.

Before long I was squawking even louder than I had plunked. My "OOPS" routine grew louder and wilder, bordering on madness in my haste to conquer my musical disability and make my mother proud. Before I could believe it, recital night hovered in the immediate future. Neither mastery of the strings nor flexibility of my fingers had occurred. Disappointment etched itself in crow's-feet surrounding my mother's sad eyes. I too was desperate. I secretly searched the musty closet in the dusty music room at school but discovered nothing new. Nothing used. Nothing at all. All hope was crushed.

But then on the Monday before the Friday night recital, an unexpected note was routed to my regular classroom, folded in half and addressed to Patsy Ann. I peeked beneath the fold and read: "Meet me in the music room after school." The signature was plain and straightforward: *Mrs. Campbell.*

I knew what was coming. My rejection to the dung heap of the musically untalented had become commonplace. But I was a year older now, nearly grown up. I could take it. I prayed Mrs. Campbell hadn't sent a duplicate note to my mother.

But Mrs. Campbell was sitting alone when I arrived. Her grand piano was bathed in the warm sunlight that flooded the polished floor of her beloved music room. She stopped practicing chords on the polished keys of the piano my mother coveted. Smiling, she stood to greet me.

"Patsy Ann! You're right on time. Good girl! I have a surprise for you! You've worked so hard searching for just the right instrument. And I think I've helped you find it. But you must make that decision." She passed a small box to me. It was cube-shaped, about four inches square, cardboard, and unadorned. Puzzled, I looked up into her sparkling eyes. A warm smile crossed her lips and she chuckled. *Was she laughing at me?* I wondered. *Was this the cruelest of all jokes? Would a frog leap out?*

"Go on. Open it. It won't bite you." Cautiously I opened the sturdy box and peeked inside. I drew in my breath as I lifted the strange object from its tissue wrap. I was unsure of how to respond. "Was I bad?" I asked. "Is it a puzzle?" Mrs. Campbell knew I hated puzzles. *Was she trying to punish me for my musical failures?*

She shook her head. "No, dear, it's not a puzzle." When she lifted it from my hands, it twinkled in the light that danced from the window. She sat down with me on the piano bench, holding the gift between us. To me it looked like a three-cornered steel rod bent in the shape of a teepee; but one corner didn't quite come together. *Sloppy workmanship*, I thought.

Mrs. Campbell's voice interrupted my thoughts: "Keep going! The best part is yet to come. Look underneath the tissue." When I did, I discovered another steel rod, this one small, short, and straight. I frowned—first at one object, then the other. Mrs. Campbell chuckled again. "It's an instrument," she said, "a percussion instrument. When I found it at Harmony Music Store, I knew it was meant for you! It's a fun instrument too! And *I'm* betting you can learn to play *this* instrument by Friday! Your mother will be so proud! I have the feeling you're going to be a great percussionist. The best in the school. Maybe the best in the country!" I was impressed by her enthusiasm and mesmerized by my newest instrument; I continued sitting on the piano bench as Mrs. Campbell stood.

"Come on. Get up," she urged. "I'll show you how it works. Then, we'll practice together." Following her triangle demonstration, she reseated herself at the piano.

I don't remember which march we practiced together in the fading afternoon sunlight—but I remember the clangs at the end of each fourth measure: My first timid peals grew with each stanza. At first just melodious, they gradually became spirited. Soon the reverberating noise exploded from my little triangle. Mine were not fool-around clangs. My clangs meant business! By the end of Mrs. Campbell's John Philip Sousa rendition, my clangs had reached ear-splitting proportion.

She kept nodding and shouting, "Good! Good! Very good!" The volume of her voice increased simultaneously with the rising volume of my emphatic staccato clangs! My drooping socks, crooked bangs, and dangling hair barrette went unnoticed. Her Sousa march ended in a final grand crescendo and my ultimate clang burst forth like fireworks into the room. Mrs. Campbell jumped up, then bent down to hug me. And in that instant, despite my diminutive stature, I felt BIG! And it felt good.

My fourth-grade vocabulary did not include the word *faith* or *encouragement*, but as an adult, when I reflect on Mrs. Campbell's gift, I realize it was neither her triangle nor my successful performance that inspired me. It was Mrs. Campbell's faith in my *ability* to succeed that created that fourth-grade miracle.

And, no, I never became a musician. And, yes, my mother loved me anyway. And I will always remember her for her musical daydreams. But I will remember Mrs. Campbell for a gift more precious than music.

I remember her when things in life get really hard. And I keep plugging along. Plugging away. Starting over.

After all, I mastered the triangle. So nothing can stop me now.

JOANNE WOODWARD
actress

— writing about —

ROBERT MACLANE
her drama teacher

My favorite teacher was an artist, a designer, a director, and a lover of theater. Mr. Robert H. MacLane taught me drama at Greenville High School in South Carolina.

He took my aspirations seriously and encouraged me in them. In my senior year Mr. MacLane cast me as St. Joan in the play *Joan of Lorraine*. He found a college for me with a good drama department and then encouraged me to attend the Neighborhood Playhouse in New York City. Mr. MacLane proved to me it was possible to have a career as an actress.

If he were here (and he died several years ago), I would say, *Thank you, Mr. MacLane, for my career.*

LOVE OF THE DANCE

*Fondly dedicated to the dancers of the Northgate High School
1989–90 dance production workshop and to Sue Pipo, who left
our world far, far too soon*

In the young midnight of life
spirits tethered to a pale rose,
a blossoming Maypole
that protects their innocent orbit,
soft, unfolding petal fire
illuminating the currents on which they glide

Love of the movement!
            Emotion of flight!
    Precise abandon!
        Courageous body strokes!
            Physical color!
Love of the dance!

And then so suddenly a broken stalk,
the rhythmic waves crash out of course,
tidal emptiness
severing the ribbons onto which they hold,
thorns pricking those smooth spirit cheeks,
teardrops and life blood moistening the stage.
Yearning for answers,

gazing into these salty, ruby pools,
a movement is detected against the starless sky,
familiar choreography, but whose?
Revealed in tears and blood, like crimson mirrors,
it is they who remain aloft,
firing the sky in graceful streams,
circling together
to generate the light of a rose within,
finally knowing a beautiful truth.
She never held them up at all,
a loving illusion to strengthen youthful wings
so they might fly.

And now they fly.
Sometimes crooked, sometimes tired,
Sometimes pure and perfect,
caressing the collective wound
to remember, always remember,
why they're here

Love of the movement!
          Emotion of flight!
   Precise abandon!
      Courageous body strokes!
         Physical color!
Love of the dance!

Jeff Spoden

PADMINI PARTHASARATHY
college student

— w r i t i n g   a b o u t —

H. T. PAYNE
her former orchestra director

The ecstasy after a superb musical performance is like no other human emotion, my teacher and conductor H. T. Payne used to say. The heart pounds and adrenaline rushes, crying for an encore. The musician wants to stand up and belt out the same powerful tones and chords once more. As life presents such ecstasy, it also presents deep sorrow. On the morning of Wednesday, April 20, 1994, Mr. Payne passed away. I tasted confusion and fear in my tears; the colors of the past, present, and future flooded together, creating a brown bewilderment.

Mr. Payne incited every musical group he ever directed. He motivated us with praise, yet told us the truth. This dedicated educator believed in all his students, including me. Though he directed four high school groups, an elementary school program, and a youth symphony, he found the time to be a devoted father, husband, and friend. His work never ended at school; students were welcome to call him or drop by his house. He loved us as his children.

In reviewing his life, many people said, "H.T. worked too much. He did too many things." On holidays and weekends, Mr. Payne could be found digging through piles of compositions at Byron Hoyt Sheet Music. Many felt the stressful life he led was responsible for his fatal heart attack. However, this zeal to be involved in any and all activities was what defined H. T. Payne as a person. The man was my hero, and I learned on that Wednesday that even heroes die.

On May 26th that year, the music students of Northgate High School performed a Memorial Concert for H. T. Payne. The fire of the Stravinsky, the thunder of Mosier, the sorrow of Grieg, the grace of Beethoven, and the grandeur of Hovhaness wrestled in my spirit for days and months to come. Now, two years later, I keep moving forward, my love and commitment to music still increasing.

Not until Mr. Payne's death did I realize what I wanted from life. From a very young age, I had a curious, persistent nature; at the age of five, I pestered my parents into letting me take violin lessons. My friends played Little League; I played Bach. Fourteen years later, through five years as a member of the Young Artists Symphony Orchestra, four years of high school orchestra, and now my first year in a university orchestra, music has become part of my very soul.

After Mr. Payne's death, I realized I should make the most of my life. Someone once warned me human nature might lure me to forget this promise of dedication, but I will never forget. Mr. Payne's passion for music is reincarnated as my own.

Now each time I achieve one of my goals, I feel that musical ecstasy. The victory proclaimed in Tchaikovsky's *1812 Overture* is *my* victory, each time a baby is born healthy or a hungry soul is fed. Cannons explode gloriously and spirits rise; my gut reaches up to nudge my throat as I smile with pride. One song ends and I prepare for the next one to begin.

STEVE ECKERT
clinical social worker

— w r i t i n g   a b o u t —

AL SALACH
his music instructor

I sent this letter last year to my most inspirational teacher, Al Salach:

You may or may not remember me, but I was a guitar student of yours for four years. I am writing to thank you for giving me not only the gift of music proficiency, but also the example to live an honest and giving life. I have wanted to write this letter for a long time; I hope that even if you have passed on, your family can read this and be reminded of how much your generosity and patience were appreciated.

Like so many kids my age who were given our allowance of British rock and roll every Sunday night by Ed Sullivan, I begged my parents for a guitar. My grandfather came through with a three-quarter-size beginner's flattop, and on my eleventh birthday I started weekly lessons with you.

Lessons were not fun. You made me learn one string at a time and conspired with my mother to make me practice every day. It was almost as bad as memorizing lines required by nuns for Saturday catechism, but you were nicer (which may have been worse). My parents wouldn't let me grow long hair and I didn't sound like the Beatles.

When I was twelve, my mother bribed me to practice, with the promise of a full-size folk guitar. You taught me folk chords so I could play simple songs for the relatives, with my sister who was also your student. I saw my first live rock band at the Grange Fair; it comprised local teenagers who may have been your students. I stood in awe in front of a very loud speaker, feeling the music physically shake my innards against my rib cage. I was hooked.

When my parents fought and threatened divorce, I took my baby brother to my room or put him in the bathtub. I played my guitar, not loud enough to divert their rage to me, but loud enough to hear sounds that *I* made, sounds that were soothing. I never was afraid of you, even though you made it clear that when I took the responsibility to practice, I played better.

When I was thirteen, you sold me my first amplifier so I could play in a garage band. This amp was your personal Fender Deluxe, which I heard you use between lessons when you played electric jazz guitar. My parents were amused that I cut such a good deal with you; I remember your wife was worried next you might sell her living room furniture that you borrowed from home for your studio office.

By the time I was fourteen, I practiced almost daily with my band. With amplifiers the size of refrigerators, we were loud, but we actually sounded like the records on the radio. We played school and church dances—and mesmerized other kids. Your opening me to music allowed me to experience not only the likes of Jimi Hendrix, but also Father Joe Rozint, who drafted me to play in his *Traveling Salvation Show* for prisons and other venues.

While my parents battled over the risks of allowing me to play, you seemed to know my playing was inevitable. You did not seem to worry about whether I played in rock bands or for the church, but insisted that honesty and genuineness characterize my endeavor. While I can't say your influence was solely responsible for my decisions, I waited longer than my friends to experiment with drugs and other dangerous behavior.

By 1970, my brother and sisters were also taking lessons with you; that was when my dad was laid off from work. When I told you we had to stop, in your typical Al Salach way, you immediately offered to give free lessons. Though my parents wouldn't allow me to accept, the generosity of your offer is forever with me. While guitar lessons wouldn't pay my parents' bills, you seemed to know we would need stability and the solace of making music.

I never became as famous as the Beatles or Jimi Hendrix, but your influence has carried me in a lot of ways. Over the years, I have jammed with new friends every time I've moved, sometimes creating bands that play actual gigs, more often just having fun. You gave me the skills to communicate with people through music. More importantly, you let me experience an adult who could insist on perseverance without rage, all the while being patient and encouraging in the step-by-step context of music lessons.

I am a clinical social worker now. When I sit in my office with a child, often abused or from a divorcing family, I am reminded of you patiently working with me, helping me master my guitar. I give my clients homework, which they some-times do, but mostly I sit and listen to them, as you listened to our music, offering encouragement and challenging them to take responsibility.

I have been seeing an eleven-year-old girl for the last four years who has had much trauma and little stability in her life. Recently her mother had to give her up to a foster home because of the mother's repeated suicide attempts. This young girl's case has been shifted from caseworker to case-worker, and she has had to change schools every year. When the government funding for her therapy with me ended, I decided to continue seeing her without compensation. My eleven-year-old client doesn't know it, but those sessions are funded by the "Al Salach Bank of Good Will."

I hope life has been good to you and your family. While I would enjoy a reply, I do not expect one. Enclosed is a pic-ture of me playing with my latest band, a group of psy-chotherapists named "5150" (Danger to Self or Others).

Thank you so much.

TEACHERS

I.
Helen Hum and Blanche Garrison have their large arm around me, and I am being pressed against the massive slope of their bosom. I am looking up at their silvery shingles of hair and their

broad roll of chin. *Don't be afraid of the paint,* says Helen Hum. *Just write what comes to mind,* Blanche Garrison adds.

II.
Miss Clementi needs to appear somewhere. With her long and coiling unwashed braids. Her Brooklyn Italian accent shrill through the French *Ici on parle francais!* Her high heels and dainty calves. Her eternal youth. Too inexperienced to understand Gide, her professor told her. So she dropped her dissertation and turned to teaching. Her icy hands and praising letter sent to my home. Pink envelope in my maple drawer: *May you always stay just as you are.*

III.
Catherine Jackson is seated at the harp. With frizzy gray hair, dangling earrings, and her long powdered nose. Long bare arms, satiny skirt with hand-painted flowers spread over her knees: *My mother said I'd never amount to a hill of beans.* Her strong callused fingers press into the strings. Then she swishes out the door, her high laugh glissandoing. Lifts her foot—the one in the elevated red leather shoe—into her yellow Jeep, and vanishes over the hill. Her handwriting swirls gaily over the page: *You can do whatever you want.*

Janine Canan
psychiatrist

MARIE HENRY
poet, writer

—— w r i t i n g   a b o u t ——

SISTER SUZANNE
her high school chorale director

SUSPENDED FROM A HIGH NOTE

Sister Suzanne was so shy when she first started directing the Mercy High School Chorale, she'd climb upstairs to the third-floor balcony, put on white gloves so the girls down below could see her hands, and conduct from up there. That was a few years before my time. We also heard that even when she eventually worked up enough courage to conduct from the auditorium floor, she stood behind a screen so the audience couldn't see her.

By the time I made my entrance into that elite group of voices, Sister Suzanne was over the worst of her timidness. Though her face still flushed whenever she turned to face the audience, at least she managed to take her proper place in front of us.

Dressed in our long blue choir gowns and high heels, we warily mounted the unsteady risers, tottering into place—sopranos, second sopranos, altos, second altos. A hum of the pitch pipe and she would gather our faces to her, raise her hands, her face alight, and draw out sounds utterly fresh and pure. Her tall, lean body disappeared in the music and she took our voices into places they had never been. Her eyes opened wide, catching up galaxies, then hushed us into whispers. Her chipmunk cheeks grew solemn, then broke into joy—held all the expressions that appeared on our faces as the music came tumbling out.

Her hands . . . her hands were full of secrets, with fingers that became seven feet long as she reached out to draw us in. She hypnotized us with those hands. Quietly led our voices into sacred places one moment, then nudged them scurrying off like squirrels through tree branches. Her fingers told us jokes and sent our voices laughing over triplets, taught us languages we somehow understood without knowing. Her hands held forty voices—scooped them up and caressed them, stretched and blended them.

The grand ballroom of the Tudor brick mansion that served as our high school auditorium held all those years of voices—floating up past the carved wooden fireplace and Renaissance mural to the third-floor balcony where her white-gloved hands once counted out measures in the dark.

When the concert was over, Sister Suzanne would turn to the audience and take her bows, blushing like a schoolgirl. Row by row, careful of our long robes and high heels, we moved along in single file, climbing down off the risers. Inevitably, one girl's shoe remained behind, stuck between a crack and a high note.

It is strange to say a dance professor taught me to taste wine and cook pasta sauce with just the right amount of garlic, but these were the tools Alice used to refine our senses and in turn, our dance style. She would bring her awareness for beauty into the dance studio and awaken her students to their surroundings. Simply by acknowledging the scent in the air, the warmth of her coffee, or the feeling of a movement, we as students began to take notice of daily life.

By sensing detail and awakening my body, I started to develop a deeper sense for choreography and purity in movement. Alice taught me to appreciate the emotion within motion. It was her enthusiasm and passion I found contagious and admired.

She was successful at pushing our notions of creativity. In a simple choreographic assignment we were to create an eight-count phrase. Once we presented our constructed movement, Alice asked us to do the phrase backwards, against a wall, lying down, in a corner. Through this exercise I saw how endless the possibilities were. It was a clear lesson in pushing myself to always ask what else could be tried. This liberation affects my thinking in all aspects of life. And all this was done through the medium of dance.

Alice would bring history and life into the dance studio and in so doing, bring dance to life. Alice's rich background included working as a member of the José Limón dance company. Limón was a choreographer whose work was influenced by Native American rituals and rhythms. The company still exists and is considered an important part of modern dance history. José has passed, but Alice continued to share his spirit and philosophies with her students.

Whenever Alice was struck by a relevant memory or thought, she would stop her instruction and share her story. I remember one time in a dark theater during a rehearsal, she suddenly stopped us and asked, "Did you hear that?" We fell silent, not sure what to listen for. "José is here," she said with a smile. She could be crazy, but this was the magical energy she brought to her surroundings. She always had a flamboyant imagination. She walked into class another day and remarked, "Wouldn't it be wonderful if we had a dance path, like the bike path. Everyone could dance their way to class." This habit of sharing her innermost thoughts enriched the point she was making; it felt as if Alice let us in on little secrets of life.

While working with her on a piece she choreographed, one rehearsal stays embedded in my mind. Using a common improvisational technique, she set up a relationship between me and two male dancers. Our role was to move with each other in accordance with our "characters." She never gave us situations we couldn't be ourselves in; this ensured our emotional responses and movement were genuine. At one point in this session I became overwhelmed with anger and sadness. Never before had physical movement pushed me to such an intense emotional state. Alice seemed to foresee this point she was directing us to. That moment was a breakthrough in my relationship to dance as a deeper art form. Although at the time I was uncomfortable, I thank Alice for pushing me into a more sincere direction of working. Since that rehearsal, performing has been a place of clarity, not coated emotion.

Although Alice taught dance, from her I learned to appreciate life. She brought the outside world and the person within, to movement. I thank her for her stories, her passion, and her harsh critical eye. She was always encouraging me to ask more questions about my work, about how I was feeling, or about how to improve dance technique. It was a good habit to form. Just by listening to Alice explain something—music, dinner, or a dance performance—I felt my senses awaken. From Alice I suppose I learned how to learn . . . and live with an openness. Besides her endless knowledge, it was her energy, voice, and crazy mind that left such an impression.

SARA SUTHERLAND
college student

— w r i t i n g   a b o u t —

ROD FIESTER
her high school choir director

I have been blessed with a good voice and lucky enough to be born into a musical family where that gift could be exercised. Mr. Rod Fiester was my conductor in various music performance activities all the way through high school; he directed the concert and pep bands. However, what will always stay with me is my involvement in music my senior year. I joined the school choir, which was under Mr. Fiester's direction.

Our choir was quite good. We did many selections a cappella, which takes great concentration. Mr. Fiester's training included performing in unconventional ways, such as singing in a ring around the auditorium. We were arranged into sections: sopranos, altos, tenors, and basses; that way the singers could hear and focus on their proper parts. The performance was a magical experience for both singers and audience: The voices meshed in the air above the assembly; the combined sound misted down. Listeners had the unique pleasure of hearing the rightness of the mix, and the clarity of whatever part they happened to be seated by. It was beautiful and something I'll never forget.

I'll also always remember Mr. Fiester's expressive conducting style. If a section of the choir was screwing up, his intense stare and furrowed brow practically screamed *Straighten up!* If the sopranos were flat, he'd raise his eyebrows; if we needed to get louder, he'd open his eyes wider and wider. The audience could never tell what an intense conductor he was. They couldn't see his eyes, which were fiery and constantly conveying his urgent messages.

I started auditioning for solos in the choir. When I sing, I tend to be a perfectionist; I like to be precise about the details in pitch and rhythm. Mr. Fiester took time to coach me individually at lunch and after class. Each time I performed on my own, I gained confidence. He had so much faith in me, it helped me gain enough confidence so I finally shared his faith. It was evident in his firm handshake and the solemn "Break a leg" he pronounced before we all went onstage. I remember once when I was in the spotlight alone, doing one of my solo songs, I looked out at the audience and saw him in the darkness of the front row. As I sang, he was nodding slightly, as if he'd known all along.

A turning point of that year came when I landed the lead female role in *The Music Man*. That musical changed my life. I had never done any acting and was plenty nervous about all I had to learn. Fortunately, Mr. Fiester was the music director for the production and was present at every rehearsal. He also worked with me and others during lunch, two or three times a week. The resounding success of that play changed the way I perceived myself and my capabilities.

It is difficult to portray Mr. Fiester's way of teaching music and why it influenced me so greatly. I just sensed his overwhelming confidence in me. I remember him telling me repeatedly, "Don't second-guess yourself—you've got it." It was a wonderfully comforting thing to fall back on when I was feeling down. I felt he held me in higher esteem than just a student; he regarded me as a fellow musician, someone with talent. I guess that's the heart of it all: He believed in me and gave me the training, the time, and the encouragement I needed to succeed. As a result, I grew to think of myself as a singer rather than some girl attempting to sing.

Mr. Fiester made an indelible impact on my life. I thank him from the bottom of my heart.

MR. HINMON

Mozartian man of
melody melancholy, in
hat, a cap: like an
English chap.

And sweater vest,
plastic coverings for shoes—
they amuse, amuse.
"Hello, Rich." ENTER HE.
"Hi, Mr. Hinmon," ANSWER ME.
Chat and chitter and titter
of movies and books—
The Thorn Birds,
Biography, Ogden Nash.
"Well, shall we?"
Yes, let's shall, let's make
Beethoven, Bach,
Lloyd Webber, Saint-Saëns—
"You know, he has the same birthday
as me."
Kind, gentle—ne'er a word of
wrongdoing, instead, "That's good,
but let's try this instead . . ."
instead.
And when it's right it's "That's

the way!"
And forty minutes later after playing, parlaying:
"Rich, I'll see you next week."
SAY I: "All right, Mr. Hinmon,
see you next week." Shake, ensure
his ensuing departure is safe and then
sit with sure sitting in mind and in seat
that the piano teacher will be back, be back
in one week.

Rich Russell
student

RUTH A. ROUFF
basic skills writer/tutor

— w r i t i n g   a b o u t —

CHRISTINE HAVELOCK
her art history teacher

It isn't that I remember much of what Professor Christine Mitchell Havelock taught me—Greek art was far from my best subject. Professor Havelock was memorable for the aura she projected in a classroom. Even today, some twenty years later, I can still see her: aristocratic, coolly intellectual, and—best of all—brazenly unfair to the men in the class.

Before you label me a Limbaughian femi-nazi, may I remind

you this was Vassar College in the mid-1970s. Only a few short years before, Vassar had decided to go coed and it was no secret Christine Havelock had been opposed to the college's decision. It wasn't that she was a man hater; she was married to the distinguished art historian Eric Havelock. It was, I think, that she believed in women.

This was easy to tell in the very first class I took with her. At her weekly seminar, we got to spout off about all the art we had seen and learned in the Art History slide presentations. Predictably the men in the class were more forthright about expressing their opinions than the women.

I remember those seminars well: Some guy would self-confidently expound his opinion on some piece of art or another. Simultaneously a look of sheer disdain would creep across Christine Mitchell Havelock's alabaster features. "Surely not," she'd respond in that clipped Canadian way of hers. "Surely not." The guys in the class were taken aback. It was so obvious she favored the women, it became hilarious. After all, it wasn't that Christine Havelock was mean or nasty in her disdain for the opinion of young men; it was that she was a bluestocking par excellence—a staunch upholder of the Vassar feminist tradition.

She wore her long, graying hair in a bun, which one of my waggish classmates dubbed "the Havelock knot," as in "there are the Havelocks and the Havelock knots." To me, she was the perfect antidote to the household I had come from: She contrasted strikingly with my mother.

Now my mother is an utterly bright woman who has lived to see six of seven children graduate from college and two go on to obtain advanced degrees. But she never went to college herself; indeed she never received any kind of encouragement to do anything with her intelligence. In her Catholic immigrant family, girls did not go to college. Girls grew up to become good Catholic wives and mothers—to have kids, *lots* of kids. So my mother lived out the plan and never did do anything with her intellect. She ironed and cleaned and cooked, and for diversion, she watched soap operas and read. And every so often, she'd explode in unarticulated frustration, slamming doors and kitchen cabinets with all her might, lashing out at us for whatever we had done wrong with disproportionate fury. To me, she was the madwoman in the kitchen. In contrast, I still can see Christine Mitchell Havelock lecturing on Praxiteles and the Temple of Zeus at Olympia, as coolly aloof as gray-eyed Athena, the Goddess of Wisdom. To me at that age, she seemed the living embodiment of female intellect and power.

CHAPTER 5

THE DANCER

*About those who made learning an
exciting, joyous experience*

Education is not the filling of a pail, but the lighting of a fire.

—*William Butler Yeats*

WISHING I COULD COUNT

For my second-grade teacher, Miss McMyrtrie

I climbed those wide, spiraled, oil-slicked stairs
cautiously early to you, moved slowly
down the musty hall, wondering how I would master
the difficult tasks: carrying, borrowing, remaindering
wishes for your bright red A's on the page,
wishing I could count
to a trillion for you, recite it, recite it
for all the class to witness, on edge,
wishing I could count
the freckles that spattered your tawny white
bosom rising up from scooped Angora, count
each strand that waved your wildly sunburnt
auburn hair. You, my Monroe and Madonna, framed
by ceiling, wall, board, clamoring cloud
of my chalky erasers, faithfully
banging the window ledge at the end of each day.
I longed for your A's, round and sure like you.
I imagined you Maureen O'Hara, whispered it
even when you made me stand
pee-soaked in my squeaking tennies on the heating grate,
even when you poisoned
my chewed nails with solution, even then
I wanted to count on them, count

your every hair and freckle, count
on them, all the way to a trillion.

Andrena Zawinski
writer, teacher

MARTHA LEY
writer, editor, photographer
— w r i t i n g   a b o u t —

RUTH LIMMER
her creative writing professor

FOR RUTH, WITH LOVE AND SQUALOR

"I won't teach a creative writing class this big," she announced. "Who wants to leave now?" No one spoke, no
one moved. She was not smiling. That's what I remember most:
Miss Limmer was not smiling.

She had burst into the room for the first class meeting and had
sat, not behind the desk, but atop it, legs swinging, rubber-soled
heels lightly tapping the oak panel as she surveyed the fourteen
of us from behind horn-rimmed glasses.

She went right on and assured us she would weed out the
faint of heart, the runts of the litter. And she did. Within two
weeks, the assignment of daily themes—with the requisite,
no-holds-barred critique from Miss Limmer—had driven five
of our classmates to the registrar's office to drop creative

writing and opt for another—*any* other—course available.

The rest of us felt pretty proud of ourselves. We were survivors. Our class now numbered only nine, and we had established a ritual of rearranging the chairs into a lopsided circle to create a more intimate seminar environment. It was an unusually warm day for late March. Bees were buzzing and bouncing off windowpanes in the sunny classroom in Alumnae Hall. We students felt overwhelming claustrophobia, yearning to be outdoors. Winter seemed over, and the last days of school beckoned at the end of a long, chalk-dusted tunnel.

Six months of writing together had forged a closely bonded group. Some of our humble scribblings had been thinly veiled autobiographical ramblings; others featured fantasy places and starred swashbucklers of our adolescent dreams.

Through the semester, some of us emerged more battle scarred than others; her class was tough. We learned—sometimes with tears—not to be attached to our prose, nor especially to our finite ways of looking at things. We were urged, cajoled, and finally when those techniques failed, *ordered* to open our eyes and look, to open our minds and see.

As well as we students thought we knew each other, our professor Miss Limmer remained elusive. She was an enigma. The real Miss Limmer, that is. Never in question were her common sense, practicality, intelligence (many said brilliance), sense of humor, extraordinary teaching ability, and wide understanding of literature and the world. Knowing all that, however, we still did not know her, the woman.

Sometimes I thought of her as unfathomable, simply too deep

to measure. I had an image of marine scientists trying to plumb her depths, watching in wonder as the winch let the line out farther, farther, and still farther—down, down, down it would go. They'd frown, scratch their heads, whistle through their teeth, and raise their eyebrows. "Never saw anything like it," an old-timer would say. "We've used all the line we have, and we still haven't reached the bottom!"

Although six months had passed by that March afternoon, I can't say I found Miss Limmer any less awesome than the autumn afternoon when I met her for the first time . . . but I had an inkling something special was taking place that seemed not only beyond words but beyond my control. It was on this day it seemed to crystallize; at last I could find words for the subtle transformation I had been experiencing.

Our assignment had been to read and study *Nine Short Stories* by J. D. Salinger. In the spotlight that particular March afternoon was "For Esme, with Love and Squalor." Some of us were called on to recount an aspect of the story that had caught our attention, but no one exhibited any particular enthusiasm. Many were just waiting absentmindedly for the liberating bell to ring; others, I suppose, wished we could talk about a different story, "A Perfect Day for Banana Fish" perhaps.

It could have been that Miss Limmer was as bored as we were with the listless discussion—I don't know why—but she began to tell us what *she* had seen in the story. As she spoke, her eyes sparkled, and a smile—such a smile—illuminated her face. She read passages from Salinger's story to illustrate her points, and she seemed about to bubble over like some marvelous concoction momentarily forgotten on the back burner of the stove.

Miss Limmer gathered me up in her smile, and then her enthusiasm swept me right into her mind and heart. I was witness to something extremely intimate; I was bestowed with a glimpse into what made this extraordinary woman love life. In that moment, I became an integral part of that frothing, bubbling stew.

Her unbounded enthusiasm sparked some neurons in my brain and, more significantly, opened my heart to life. I wanted more. I wanted to know what could move a person so. That afternoon Miss Limmer showed me that such passion, such engagement, was possible; and I wanted to experience it, to engage with it fully in my own heart.

Her self-revelation in class that day was, for me, a call to action—a summons that miraculously reached and touched my heart and mind. So, for all the subsequent love and squalor in my life—every precious moment of it since 1962—I respectfully and lovingly dedicate this to Ruth Limmer, Professor of English, Western College, Oxford, Ohio.

MAL SINGER
high school physics and math teacher

— w r i t i n g   a b o u t —

LOUIS LOVE
his twelfth-grade physics teacher

Mr. Love lived and breathed and ate and spat out physics to his students. He made every class come alive with his enthusiasm. He would derive a formula on the blackboard and then stand back, point at it, and exclaim, "Do you see the *power* in that formula?!" And then he would show us what amazing, heretofore-taken-for-granted physics law was described by the formula.

He was the only teacher I ever had who addressed each student as Mr. or Miss. He was friendly but didn't try to become close to any of us, so to me he was a pure physics teacher; he didn't seem to exist outside that realm. We definitely appreciated his filtering out our mistakes before a test counted. You could bring your test paper up for him to look over and he'd say, "Looks good, Mr. Singer, but I'd check that third step in problem two."

Mr. Love made me love physics. It seemed like the only subject describing everything you saw and felt around you. He made it seem like the most worthy subject to devote my life to. Because of him, that's just what I planned to do. When he taught us that no one knew whether light traveled as a particle or wave, I decided I would one day be the one to discover the answer. He made me dream of getting a Ph.D. in physics.

Unfortunately Mr. Love almost led to my downfall. Because of him, I majored in physics at Cornell, even though deep inside I knew the anthropology course I took freshman year was more to my liking and ability. For four years, I struggled and competed with geniuses; I spent all my time in the library trying desperately to get Bs and Cs in a subject that seemed to relate less and less to the real world. I had such momentum from my twelfth-grade teacher that I overlooked the fact that I should have been an anthropologist instead of a physicist. I stubbornly stuck to physics and even applied and got accepted to graduate programs to do that Ph.D. But I also applied to the Peace Corps, and on that day, during the spring of my senior year when the telegram arrived inviting me to spend two years in Ghana, I knew that was what I wanted to do—and never again thought about pursuing a career in physics.

Instead I became a physics and mathematics teacher, which I've been for twenty-six years now. Louis Love is still my inspiration, both for his qualities as a teacher and for the subject he taught.

HIGH-SCHOOL CLASSICS

For Marion Klobucher

When she got serious,
we squirmed under that look,
what we were sure it saw.

She held each indifference
to Oedipus and Jocasta, Aeneas and Dido,
like an orange waiting to be peeled
and undid our too practical doubts
until we went all shy
trapped into revealing
the plots we lived by.
She met us there open-handed,
turned our stumbling common,
and admired where we arrived.

I think she admired most
the witches in *Macbeth*.
The cracks in her voice
when she read their parts
ambushed every wayward thought
until she opened up such a space
we all fell in, even the clock,
the trees outside waving wildly
for our green attentions.

We were led book by book to a house
of people with shadows in their clothes,
a voice behind the voice we heard.
We went where she went
for an hour every day.
But only a few images, a few words,

like illumined pages of our stories,
went with us.

The world, now, stops unexpectedly—
a crackled laugh, a scowl crumbling
into kindness—if what we moved from
became a part of what we are,
and she was the future
we never saw happening.

Joseph Powell
teacher

SUMANA JOTHI
medical student

— w r i t i n g   a b o u t —

SEDA CHAVDARIAN
her college French teacher

When I think of Seda Chavdarian—Madame Chavdarian—I picture her bright smiling face bursting through the door each morning with a happy *"Bonjour, classe! Comment allez-vous?"* Madame Chavdarian taught me French at the University of California at Berkeley for two consecutive semesters.

She used to call the classroom door *"La Porte Magique"* (The Magic Door), explaining to us on the first day of class that all fatigue, worries, stress, irritation, or other negative sentiment must be left outside. Once we walked into the class, she expected us to be as enthusiastic and engrossed in the beauty of the French language as she was. Although it was sometimes difficult to leave our lives outside the door, it was an amazing psychological tool for getting our minds focused on the French literature or grammar of the day. *La Porte Magique* also came to symbolize a one-hour escape from our busy, stress-filled days.

We found it hard not to give back the same effort and enthusiasm Madame Chavdarian offered us, as she always abided by her own rule. I remember one class in which she was her usual enthusiastic self throughout the lesson, but afterward told a few of us that her close friend had died the night before. She was a different person for that moment, and I suddenly gained even more respect for her commitment to our class and to her responsibility as a teacher.

Just as important as her love for the subject was her efficiency in running a class. A teacher has the choice and the authority either to impart knowledge in a non-interactive manner by simply lecturing, or to prod students with a question or insight that stimulates thinking and learning. Madame Chavdarian achieved a perfect balance between the two.

In every single class each student was given a chance to speak. Although a handful of vociferous students were always willing to volunteer comments or answers, Madame made a point of involving even the quiet students, encouraging them individually to participate. In this way, we interacted with fellow students and learned others' viewpoints, an opportunity rarely found at the college level. Madame made sure we learned as much from each other as we did from her lectures and the texts.

Seda Chavdarian will always stand out when I think of my college years. In a university like Berkeley that is so large one often feels lost in classes, Madame Chavdarian made us feel like individuals for perhaps the first time since our enrollment. The little things she did made us all feel at ease. She was always positive and encouraging. I was so surprised one day when I walked into class with a new hairdo; she noticed and complimented me in front of the class. I have yet to find a professor as effective and at the same time as warm and genuine as Madame Chavdarian.

DAN JANSEN
Olympic Gold Medal speed skater
— w r i t i n g   a b o u t —
KEN JUREK
his sixth-grade teacher

My favorite teacher from my school years was Ken Jurek. He was my sixth-grade teacher at Jefferson Elementary School in West Allis, Wisconsin. Every day he made learning fun. He also did things with us during his free time, like taking students swimming and camping. He was not like all the other teachers, but more like a friend.

PS 3558 .E85 B76 1988

For Bill Heyen

Nine years your book has rested
on its narrow wedge of metal shelf,
negligible in dimensions, unread,
seemingly untouched, since one
of our quite methodical librarians
pasted in its bar code, Dewey Decimal
numbers, & the blank Due Date slip
stamped for the first time this day,
this morning, when I cracked it open
and the words of poems exploded worlds
of geese & redwings, a
snake, jack-in-the-pulpit, milkweed
& billions of grassblades. Pages
blossomed for the first time before
my eyes, breathing me alive in time.

Karla Linn Merrifield
*director of marketing
communications at
State University of
New York at Brockport*

ADAM HACKETT
college student

—— w r i t i n g   a b o u t ——

TED ARDEN
his junior high school world civilizations teacher

OUT OF THE CLASSROOM AND INTO THE JUNGLE

"I think I *found* something, you guys!"

My classmates all rushed over to where I frantically but cautiously brushed away the sand to reveal the unidentified treasure beneath. I couldn't tell what it was, maybe a human skeleton, maybe an ancient tool, or perhaps some valuable jewelry. Grain by grain, I moved the sand away as my heart raced wildly and the others breathed down my neck.

"What is it?" an ecstatic voice quivered from behind me.

I could tell it was definitely a bone of some sort, but it had been carved and shaped for some purpose. As I exposed more and more of the hidden wonder, I tried to keep calm and steady, so as not to damage it by hurrying it out of the ground. Then I saw the blade. It was made of a black shiny stone. I had discovered a knife used by prehistoric people, and it appeared to be in excellent condition. More importantly, I had discovered an ancient civilization; where you find one artifact made by people, you are bound to find more. I learned this in my Social Stud—

R R R R R R R R R R R R R I I I I I I I I I I I I I I - INNNNNNNNNNGGGGGGGG!

I jumped as the bell jerked me back into Mr. Arden's seventh-grade Social Studies class. I stretched, brushed the sand off my jeans, and headed for the next class. As we walked out the door, I heard him say, "Remember, class, tomorrow we spend a day with the Kalahari Bushmen, so remember to pack well for our safari."

As a game show host, a dead president, a Kalahari Bushman, a radio broadcaster, an archeologist, a translator of ancient languages, and—most importantly—a teacher, Ted Arden had the ability to take a classroom of seventh and eighth graders on unforgettable journeys. He was definitely the most memorable and the most crazy-at-times teacher I ever had.

Mr. Arden made learning fun with the enthusiasm and energy he brought to teaching. More importantly, he got his students involved; he made us *want* to learn. His teaching inspired me to participate; I did hours of research and project work. By the time the year was over, I felt as if I had been on an archeological dig, to the Sahara Desert to see the Bushmen, to ancient Egypt to build a pyramid. I had learned to read and write hieroglyphics.

I will never forget what I learned in that class. It wasn't the material that was so important, but the style in which I learned. While Ted Arden provided excellent spoken information, he also always furnished visual aids and hands-on work in class and at home. With these three methods of presenting information—auditory, visual, and kinesthetic—everyone was able to learn in the way that suited them best.

I have been in school for the past sixteen years, and I've had dozens of teachers, but none have been as enthusiastic and exciting as Mr. Arden. I will always remember his passion for teaching. He had a way of brightening up the classroom, of taking us to another place in our minds: out of the classroom—and into the jungle.

ROBERT WOLLEY
retired teacher

—— writing about ——

MISS KELLEY
his high school history teacher

"Mark my word," my mother said in response to my complaint about the old, frazzled, punitive woman teacher. (My mother always was demanding that I mark her words.) "You will learn something from her and remember it the rest of your life." I marked the words, or at least I promised to. Mother was right. To this day, fifty-five years later, I not only remember many things, I can still vividly see "Pegleg" Kelley getting them across to us.

When I got to high school, Ancient History was a required subject; Miss Kelley was the teacher. She was old, she was frail, and she had an artificial leg.

The first few days of class testified to her age. She appeared worn out and hanging on until retirement. But it soon became apparent her frailty was deceiving. She ruled her classroom with a seemingly unbreakable yardstick. A tap to get your attention could be—sometimes was—followed by a compelling rap. She came across as Attila the Hun.

It was all-out war for a few days: the rigid Spartan vs. the freedom-loving Athenians, and the only weapon the students had was Miss Kelley's peg leg. Out of her hearing, we called her "Pegleg" Kelley. We retaliated against her discipline by making jokes among ourselves because most of our parents had had Miss Kelley and counted her as one of the shining personages of their school years.

Then a remarkable thing happened in her classroom: Miss Kelley established control of a bunch of history-ignorant malcontents and began leading us on a journey. And in the process she came alive.

After just three or four days of carefully orchestrated riot control, we were living in Grecian houses and theaters, on the battlefield, in the senate, first in Athens, then in Sparta. She was a general leading troops into battle, a protagonist for this idea or that, and if not in Greece, then in Gaul and Egypt, Rome and Britain.

Miss Kelley was an animated spirit, dancing with the joys of comedy, crying the anguish of tragedy. She drew us in, made us part of the human drama. We sketched maps and pictures, made models, read, and learned the art of debate. We played the role of gods and goddesses, acted out the lives of humans; we experienced history as a living, breathing, ongoing process in which we were a living, breathing part. Ancient history became as immediate as yesterday with all its mistakes and cruelties and stupidities and with all its wondrous progress and people of sublime humanity.

It was over all too soon. We were exhausted from the mad rush through thousands of years of human struggles. Without exception, all of us would have continued on for another year. What Miss Kelley gave us was an awareness of the grand sweep of history as made by men and women and a sense of our place in that sweep; she made us feel the fundamental impulse of the human drive toward goodness and made us see that history is being made every day, some of it by us.

Miss Kelley retired and died before the horrors of World War II were fully revealed. I don't know what she would have made of that. Some of what she taught us has been proven incorrect by more modern scholarship and research; she would have been the first to embrace the new truths. There are some things she never told us. For instance, she never told us that recess and gym, in Spartan schools, were conducted as coeducational activities in the nude—whatever the weather. And Miss Kelley never told us Spartan men were expected to be actively bisexual, married or not. She neglected to mention the moral depravity of the Vikings. She ignored some of ancient history's greatest civilizations and accomplishments: Phoenicia, China, and Japan. Ancient history was, in the mode of her day, Western civilization, meaning Rome and thereafter, but with Egypt and Greece thrown in. Even the Moors were shortchanged, the bad guys, with the Crusades told only from the Christian point of view.

But Miss Kelley never fell into the trap, so common then and today, of labeling everyone who believed differently as a pagan. Miss Kelley attended my Universalist church occasionally. My friends said they saw her often in their Baptist, Catholic, Congregational, and Methodist churches, and in the temple. She became a remarkable presence, once we came to know her, a woman of universal awareness and with a catholic regard for all human faiths and endeavors.

After all, who else would shed honest-to-goodness tears when describing the burning of Alexander the Great's library, become a cheerleader for the aborted attempt by the Pharaoh Akhenaton to establish monotheism in Egypt (700–600 years before Judaism "discovered" one God), lead us into the wondrous world of Michelangelo's "Creation," draw us into the marvelous engineering feats of the Roman builders, allow us to see through the Greek tragedies the limits of both deities and humans?

Miss Kelley's history was not of dates and wars; it was Egyptian water-moving devices, Roman arches, Greek plays; it was Egyptian slaves, Greek citizens, Roman soldiers—their lives, homes, families, religions. Miss Kelley was Socrates teaching by example and asking the kinds of questions that demanded research and thinking.

With scissors, cardboard, and glue we reconstructed ancient homes and temples; with papier-mâché we re-created the world (or at least a part of it); with balsa wood we reproduced weapons and tools. Some of us wore togas, noble Romans; some of us were Celts in homespun and furs. We were "the people who came before"; we were the people who came after.

People are history; that was Miss Kelley's message: struggling, striving people—struggling to survive, seeking the best life possible, striving to achieve the better life—common, everyday people from whose ranks came the shakers and shapers of history, from whose ranks might come today's and tomorrow's leaders and movers. There might be an important person among us; even if not, we were to remember our duties as citizens and our obligations as human beings to be forces for good.

Religious tolerance and political democracy were sacred ideals; continued learning and an open mind were sacred obligations; living for the betterment of humankind was a sacred duty. The sacred and the secular were indistinguishable in her sense of life because life was sacred.

Miss Kelley taught us all that in public school more than fifty years ago. I tell *you* all this because sometimes we need to be reminded of the things we learned long, long ago.

MOTHER'S LATIN

You preferred the exotic in that raw town,
a kitchen on Second Avenue South.
Your gift of strange words:
verdant, columbarium, cum laude.
One hand an actress sweeping air,
the other tucked in pinafore.
Veni, vidi, vici, you recited verbatim
near white curtains of potato steam.
We kicked each other at the table
but your language followed us.

Mother, we never believed Roman gods
left white drifts on the fence
or our casserole was wild boar.
When you became Cicero, we rolled our eyes,
little slaves with chores.

Your voice was all.
Ear learns from ear.
Those odd words, your indefatigable supply—
some days, Shakespeare's iambic round your head
as coffee boiled away on the old gas stove.
Ouside, a glad wren.

Baths, then. Embroidered gowns, red and classical
up the creaky stairs. Below, we heard Caesar
in a mother's voice: *Quo vadis?*
Soon he'll be bound in triple chains,
your monologue to pots and pans.

We were small syllables in a wooden bed,
foot to foot. You called *Equus* and hooves
galloped in our ears. We rode into the night
sky, its familiar alphabet of stars
which still spells *amo, amas, amat.*

Maureen Micus Crisick
*instructor at the University of
Phoenix (poem first appeared
in* The Nebraska Review)

CHAPTER 6

THE BELIEVER

*About those who pushed students
to find inner strength and
determination*

Education is what happens to the other person,
not what comes out of the mouth of the educator.
—*Miles Horton*

DUMMIES

The year I was promoted,
They renamed grades 4A and 4B
To 4 North and 4 South
So us dummies would not feel
Inferior to the students
Who progressed from 3A to 4 North.
That may have fooled parents
Who weren't interested in what
Was happening to their offspring
But it never fooled us dummies.
We knew A was better than B
And North was up and South was down.
Maybe we didn't learn as fast
But we weren't stupid.

Miss Murphy taught 4B that year.
She was a small, animated lady
Who darted and flitted
about the room.
To us kids she was old, old, old.
Maybe she was over forty, almost.

We learned about Africa and the Congo,
China and the Great Wall,
In Miss Murphy's fourth-grade Geography.

We learned our multiplication tables
In the hour we studied Arithmetic,
We stood and recited
2 x 2 all the way to 12 x 12
Until we got them all right.
We not only learned multiplication,
We learned to spell it and lots of other words.

Miss Murphy introduced us to literature
And Poe and poetry.
She read "The Bells" to the class.
"Keeping time, time, time,
In a sort of Runic rhyme,
To the tintinnabulation that so musically wells
from the bells, bells, bells, bells,
Bells, bells, bells."
That amazing lady, in her lilting voice,
Gave a different timbre and tone
To each and every bell.
A spellbound class
Knew magic was being performed.
We also knew that
4 North might have the smart kids
But 4 South had the smartest teacher.
Somehow that made things even.

Ain't it a shame?
Mable Murphy in Grade 4 South,

In the old Webster Building,
Taught us dummies things
Kids today,
graduating from High School,
Don't know.

> Carl Morris
> *retired postal clerk*

RICHARD RILEY
Secretary, U.S. Department of Education

—— w r i t i n g   a b o u t ——

BESS ALLEN
his third-grade teacher

 One day my third-grade class was sitting in the auditorium listening to a student who later became a concert pianist. At the time I was struggling with piano lessons. Miss Allen leaned over to me and whispered, "Dick, if you work hard and practice, you too could play like that." That kind of overwhelmed me, and I have never forgotten those words. I never had any idea I could come anywhere close to that; her comment alerted me to my potential. To this day I remember her challenge and how it encouraged me.

I am sure she had the same effect on other students over the years. If I had the opportunity to see Miss Allen again, I would thank her on behalf of all of us who benefitted from her encouragement and dedication to excellence in education. I would want her to know she played a vital part in shaping my life during the critical years: Her devotion helped raise my hopes and dreams.

OUR MISS BEMIS

Her hair was the color
of new-grown autumn leaves
short and smart
like city folk wore
she wasn't like all
the others
the women I knew
the mothers, the aunties
the grandmothers old and wrinkled down
there were none like
our Miss Bemis in that town
or the next stop along the road
a city gal she was
clear as a country sky
It was fifth grade
when she burst into
our little lives
her smile painting our

world of best friends, cherry phosphates
and tether ball
those shy girls
I was one she drew out like
honey from the nest
made us feel 100 percent
cotton new
how we wanted to please
our poetic princess
to fire up that
delicious twinkle
in her glass-covered eyes
one dark day I deceived her
passing notes across
the aisle
how I wanted to crawl
far into the whitest wall
the look of sternness
will follow me
through all the rooms
of my life
still she did forgive
me more than I ever did myself
when that hot June summer
afternoon came spiraling upon us
the day of unglad good-byes
how we cried those salty sailor's tears
we'd lost our dear Miss Bemis

to young strangers
waiting in the wings
how sorry sad our hearts were then
how empty seemed that big blue country sky

J. L. Butler
artist, teacher of creative arts

SUSAN LARSON
writer

—— w r i t i n g   a b o u t ——

JACK
her fifth-grade bus driver

"Can you take a little constructive criticism?" the editor asked about my article. As a beginning freelancer, I appreciated an editor who would take the time to offer advice. Any comment, even if negative, coming from a human voice would be more than welcome after months of finding my mailbox full of courteous little messages like "Thank you for submitting your article. We read it with interest but regret we will not be able to use it" or "Your article does not meet our editorial needs at this time."

"Don't be afraid to criticize anything I send you. I have no formal training. I just sit down and write," I confessed. I was tempted to add, "But you don't know Jack," but my better judgment told me that might take a little explaining. When it comes to writing tips, I can remember only one.

When I was in fifth grade, we got a new bus driver named Jack. Unlike most of the beer-gutted bald guys with tobacco stains on their teeth who drove school buses, Jack was the most incredibly gorgeous hunk I had ever seen in my ten years of living. And he had a sense of wit that far surpassed his good looks.

It was my first experience with a love-hate relationship. I had the biggest crush on this guy that my ten-year-old heart could bear, but his guff ignited a fury in me that made my mouth want to burst. And it did. I started mouthing right back at him every time he hurled insults at us kids, and the next thing I knew, it became a personal thing just between the two of us. If I had been Jack, I would have kicked me off the bus. I would never have taken such lip from a ten-year-old, but he seemed to thrive on it. We just fed each other insults, eagerly lapping up everything the other dished out. I hated him. And every time I felt my heart beat faster, I hated him even more.

One day I decided I hated him so much I couldn't even speak to him anymore. So I wrote him a letter. I sat down with my dictionary, tracked down synonyms, then told him in writing what an odious, obnoxious, abominable, antagonizing jerk he was. The next day I handed it to him in the afternoon as I was getting off the bus. The following morning I ignored him as I got on. That afternoon when we got to my stop, as I walked past him, he calmly said, "Susan, stay here a minute."

He unfolded my letter and said, "You're a good writer. Your grammar, punctuation, and structure are all very good. You just use too many adjectives and they cloud the meaning of what you're trying to say." He pointed to one sentence and ran his finger along all the superfluous words. "I'd like to see you rewrite this and show it to me tomorrow," he said in the kindest tone I had ever heard from anybody.

I couldn't believe it. This jerk left me speechless. I hated him! Then to fill in the gap left by my mouth, he said, "I know what I'm talking about. I'm working on a master's degree in English. I'm just driving this bus to help pay my way. I hope to be a professional writer someday."

Now, whenever I write, especially when I get carried away with adjectives and alliteration, the only thing I ever ask myself is, *What would Jack think?* And somehow I always seem to know.

But then, I know Jack.

MY SPIRITUAL LIFE

Brother Camillus gave us
an inspiring Easter talk—
how he once left the brotherhood
filled with passion for a woman
and raging against God
until he was stopped one day
by a vision.
"I saw Christ carrying his crucifix,
streams of blood carved his cheeks.

He said to me, 'I have done all this.
What have you done?'"

And Camillus returned to his faith,
his calling,
which magnified before our little group
of meditators.
He then played for us a tape
of joyful, spiritual music,
then a baroque adagio for strings
and an image rose before me—
What was it? The sacred heart?
No, it was a sandwich,
a giant hero sandwich!
I was starving: it was lunchtime.
I had no snack.
And da Vinci's "Last Supper" flashed
before me.
What were they eating?
Were there any grapes?

I felt ashamed
that the spirit had not moved me—
removed the hollow pit in my stomach
until Brother Camillus asked me later
what I had seen in my meditation.
"A sandwich," I confessed
with the honesty of a Catholic schoolgirl,
though I knew he had a sense of humor.

He laughed. "You know what Gandhi
said about the hungry poor—
The first spiritual vision
they will have is a loaf of bread!"
He moved on, but I knew then
my spiritual life
was right on target.

Judy Wells
academic counselor, poet

JAMIE ASHIMINE
graduate student, public health
— w r i t i n g   a b o u t —
RODNEY CENTENO
her swim coach

I have been a competitive swimmer since I was five. Until
the age of seventeen, I was never what one would call a
star. I swam breaststroke and occasionally freestyle, but my
coaches never put me in any other events because I never won. I
was always the kid who came in third, fourth, or even last. The
coaches would never come looking for me to swim in their star
or A relays because I just wasn't fast enough.

I thought I would always stay in the background and swim the
same events for the rest of my days until I met Rodney Centeno.

Rodney taught me how to be truly part of a team and he made *everyone* swim *everything*. He was not obsessed with winning like all other coaches I had; he wanted us to *experience* swimming.

Rodney's vigorous practice schedules (two hours before school and two hours after) taught me how to organize my time wisely, and work hard at practice and at school to better myself. Learning time management in high school gives a student tremendous advantage in college.

Rodney was constantly ready to motivate—even at 5:30 in the morning. At the time, I found his cheering painful because I did not think I could push myself any further, but in hindsight, it was important. Rodney would work out with us sometimes, which reinforced our sense of being a team.

One race was a turning point in my thinking: Every week Rodney would create a roster with everyone's names and the events we would be swimming in the meets that week. One day I looked on the roster and saw I was to swim a 500-meter freestyle, a 20-lap race. I just about had heart failure, but I said nothing to Rodney. The day of the meet, my fear of coming in ten minutes after everyone else was overwhelming. I approached Rodney and said, "Rodney, I can't swim the 500; I'll lose." Rodney responded, "I don't care if you win or lose. I want you to experience swimming it, just once." I could not believe what I had heard: He did not care if I came in an *hour* later.

I walked up onto the starting block; my lane was right next to the wall. I was petrified. Through all 20 laps, Rodney walked back and forth with me while I swam, cheering me on the whole time. Not only didn't I come in ten minutes after everyone else,

I was not even last. I found out the 500-meter was not the horrible monster of a race I had imagined.

Rodney had just given me my first lesson in trying something I knew I might not succeed at, doing it just for the experience. I learned winning did not always come from being first, but rather from knowing I did my best. I have been able to apply this to the academic part of my life: I know when I face an exam, if I have studied hard and done my work, I cannot fail—and I never have.

The summer after my first season with Rodney, I had the best summer swim season ever. With a more positive attitude and a different view on winning, I bettered my times all summer and went to the county swim championships.

I think Rodney also may have had a hand in my taking on medicine as a career goal. Many people have told me what a hard path I have chosen and that I would be safer choosing a different goal, but medicine is important to me; it is what I want to do. I know I may not become the world's best doctor, but I do know I will try my hardest and that is what is important.

Rodney was a model coach. He believed in his athletes and gave his all. When kids see that an elder or someone they respect believes anything is possible, they start to believe it too. Then dreams are born. Rodney believed in me and thus I learned to believe and trust in myself.

I never thanked Rodney and I wish I could today. I would ask him to talk to other sports coaches about the value of positive reinforcement and motivation.

WHY NOT BLOSSOM INSTEAD?

The natural world is a spiritual house—
intimate as skin, made of
evening light, purple stars,
invisible poets whose voices reach me
through tiny petalled mikes.
I'm speaking with William Stafford again.

He says what I need to hear: "It's okay
that you didn't win the Poetry Series—
                                why hang your ego
on that hook? Why not blossom lightly
from a pink dogwood?" Dutifully
I protest that I'm Jewish,
the dogwood is linked to the story of Christ.

"Trees are non-denominational,"
he laughs. He's as real to me as this
bed of wildflowers, this late sun pale and warm,
a goblet of apricot liqueur.

A river of violets answers when I look for
                                more of him.
I turn to the flowers for advice
an old friend might have offered.
An unusual animal chirps from the grass:

"So, your husband wanted this
victory for you? Whisper the truth
over him. Make corsages
of it, make forests filled with mutual sprays
of untamed blooms.
Call the wildest orchid *Losing*."

Marilyn Kallet
professor of English
(*from* How to Get Heat
Without Fire, *1996*)

ARA PARSEGHIAN
former football coach, Notre Dame University

— w r i t i n g   a b o u t —

FRANK WARGO
his high school football coach

I had great parental guidance; my parents set the standard
for moral and ethical behavior and emphasized the importance of education. But once a youngster starts school, he spends
the entire day with a teacher or coach, and that person has a
huge influence over him. Coach Frank "Doc" Wargo from
Akron South High School was that person for me.

In a public city school during the post-depression years, everyone had to make do because of limited resources. Unlike today

where teachers have one primary responsibility, teachers back then had multiple tasks. Coach Wargo served as the Athletic Director, taught Physical Education, coached football and basketball, made all travel arrangements for the teams, and acted as equipment man, trainer, and team doctor. We had no seating capacity in our own gym, so every basketball game was on the road, yet our teams were highly successful. He scheduled games at schools throughout the state, so we traveled by car and bus as far as 250 miles.

Can you imagine what I experienced while traveling with the team? No one ate out in those days. He taught us how to handle ourselves in all situations: traveling in buses and cars, staying in hotels, eating in restaurants, experiencing a life that was foreign to me.

On one long bus trip, our coach stopped in Columbus. He made arrangements for us to watch the Ohio State University football team practice and then took us to the penitentiary. What an experience! As we toured the jail, one of my teammates greeted a prisoner, a former friend who was now behind bars. That experience had a tremendous impact on me: It convinced me I would never, ever do anything to be incarcerated.

A young teenager playing for Coach Wargo generated enormous respect for his triumph over adverse conditions. He taught us what hard work was by his example. He was an outstanding coach and a great disciplinarian, traits we assimilated and used later in life.

Coach Wargo taught me many lessons of life when I was young and impressionable, and I am grateful. He was truly a teacher, a coach, and a father figure. I remember him to this day.

RAY HIMMELMAN
Sign Language interpreter

— w r i t i n g   a b o u t —

STACY INGRAM
his interpreter training instructor

My sexual orientation is an inseparable part of me I spent years learning to hate, years trying to change, and finally, years learning to accept.

For the first twenty-some years of my life, I maintained a certain psychological distance from teachers, counselors, and other adults. This emotional distance did not result from any conscious decision on my part; growing up, I was not always aware of my sexual orientation, but often had feelings I knew I was not supposed to have. But by the time I was in high school, I realized the label "gay" was relevant to me.

I had also discerned by then I was not okay. I had learned how strange and sick gay people were supposed to be, and how much my parents might blame themselves. Although I had heard religious people say my feelings were, to some extent, acceptable to God, I had also been told, in order not to sin, I would have to control myself by not acting out these feelings. Every day such messages only reinforced my negative self-image; after all, damaged goods are damaged goods, regardless of whether or not one hides the problem.

Now, at thirty-two years old, I am more comfortable with my sexual orientation than I have ever been, although I can't say I am glad to be gay. Actually, for as long as I can remember, this aspect of my life diminished my self-esteem and impeded its development. Consequently, I always felt my teachers did not know who I was. I never really trusted how my teachers reacted to me. *After all,* I always thought, *they wouldn't like me if they knew. . . .*

Today, I am "out" to my friends, family, and certain coworkers. I now have straight friends as well as gay, lesbian, and bisexual friends. I am involved in several organizations that provide me with peer support, role models, and enjoyable social activities. Although I have "come out" to some instructors and mentors in recent years, I have always had concerns about being rejected. But I never felt any of that with Stacy Ingram. Stacy is an instructor for an interpreter training program in the Midwest and a nationally certified Sign Language interpreter.

I am not sure whether Stacy knows I am gay; her knowing or not knowing, however, is not the point. I could really connect with Stacy because I sensed that sexual orientation is not an issue for her. Although she is not gay, she clearly likes and respects gay people, just as she likes and respects straight people. As her student, therefore, I always felt what she said to me was genuine. Whenever she told me I was doing well, I could not just dismiss it with my former distancing mechanism: *If she only knew. . . .* I am certain if Stacy found out about my gay orientation, she would still have the same positive regard for me and for my work she has always had.

I have often heard straight people say that gay and lesbian people should not advertise their sexuality, and should keep their personal lives to themselves. Thanks to Stacy Ingram, I now have a reasonable rebuttal: If, while growing up, I could have *felt* valued for who I was by the significant adults in my life—parents, teachers, counselors, religious leaders—I am sure I would have been a happier and healthier person.

Stacy has many attributes I like, respect, and try to emulate. She always infuses her instruction with a great deal of energy, enthusiasm, creativity, and humor. Not surprisingly, I once heard her ask, "If you don't like what you're doing, why continue doing it?"

While presenting information in organized and meaningful ways in class, she also skillfully responds to students' needs, questions, and current levels of understanding. She is clearly invested in the development of each of her students—both at the high school and college levels. Not only does she make students feel comfortable to take risks, she responds empathetically, and always has time to give individual attention where needed.

An accomplished and experienced Sign Language interpreter, Stacy Ingram frequently uses her rich background and experience to illustrate important points, and to make her lectures vivid. She respects different types of people and shows genuine interest in history, language, culture, education, psychology, physical science, and other human endeavors.

Stacy Ingram has had a profound impact on my life and helped me create a vision of the professional I want to be.

ODE ON A BALTIMORE BEA

For my grandmother Bessie Katz

I was her princess; she was my teacher.
I was hope fulfilled; she was my inspiration.
I lived well on the fruits of others' labor; she was a toiler.
I am the beneficiary of generations of women striving for equality;
    she was a pioneer.
I am the granddaughter of what was an avid intelligence,
a searing force of personality, a dogged fighter, and a vain beauty.
She was the feared, respected, admired, and—yes—
loved daughter of my namesake and mother of my own.

Ronni Baer

CHAPTER 7

THE GUIDE

*About those who helped students
find their life calling*

The art of teaching is the art of assisting discovery.
—*Pablo Casals*

TED ARDEN
teacher

—— w r i t i n g a b o u t ——

GEORGE STOKES
his history teacher

Mr. Stokes' distinguishing physical characteristic was having only one arm. He had apparently lost it in WWII; it had been replaced by a hook that served him well. On the very first day of class, I was impressed by how he dealt with his disability. He said, "I know you have a lot of questions about this, so let me show you how it works." He took off the hook in front of us all and showed us his stump of an arm. He then showed how he put the harness on and how the arm worked. We stared with a strange mixture of fear, curiosity, and awe as he demonstrated how the little cables actually moved the hook, allowing him to pick up a piece of chalk and write on the board. It was like magic, and any discomfort that had existed in the room was completely diffused.

He remained open about the prosthesis from that point on, and I never once heard any comments about it from students. I believe that's why he showed us the very first day; he wanted to confront the issue immediately and help us become more comfortable with it. He defused all our curiosity and took the freakishness away. He was the only teacher I had ever encountered with a disability who never let the problem get in the way of his teaching. That was my first impression of the man.

I had Mr. Stokes for both World History and U.S. History, and

I have many wonderful memories from each. In 1956 I fell in the gym and broke my wrist. He went out of his way for me: He allowed me to take an oral test because I could not write. He was the only teacher I ever knew who did that. I answered the questions well and got an A—and I also made an important discovery about myself: I was actually better at oral communication than writing. This led me to speech, debate, and Junior Statesmen. It was really an opening for me, and I walked through it toward my eventual profession. I also modeled my style of teaching after his; he had a powerful, dynamic voice that was interesting to listen to and could keep the attention of even the most complacent students. It was impossible not to listen.

My interest in current events was also stimulated in his classes. I remember in 1956 when the Suez Canal incident and the Hungarian Revolution took place. We discussed these in class and I found this an exciting time politically. Just the fact he was so interested in world events influenced me; he literally stopped teaching American History to talk about what was going on. He made sure we really lived through the events I would later be teaching about in my own classes. In the mid-'50s that wasn't so common.

Nor was it common in the thick of the Cold War to be liberal and to get people involved politically. I came from a conservative Republican background in a time when the suburbs of Oakland were predominantly Republican. George Stokes was a Democrat, and he let us know it. That was okay, because we could challenge him and he really enjoyed an exchange of ideas and philosophies. For example, we all knew he supported Adlai Stevenson. I was behind Eisenhower and engaged him in some lively debate over it. I could back up my arguments because he regularly had us cut out newspaper articles about the election. It was nice to have a teacher who wasn't afraid to let people know his politics, but who still honored and encouraged the expression of every student's individual beliefs.

His most important question was WHY? and he used it often. Remember, the 1950s were not WHY times. They were more about acceptance than challenge. But he would challenge us and expect us to reciprocate. My guess is that just as he challenged us not to accept the system so blindly, so he made his students of the late 1960s explain WHY they rejected it. The year after I had Mr. Stokes, I was down the hall in a class, but I could still hear Stokes, in his booming voice, probing his students with the ongoing WHY, an emotional WHY that jolted us into thinking. Above all, he wanted us to *think* in a time of less-than-vigorous analysis—and he valued the insights we offered him.

Fortunately, I had the opportunity to tell George Stokes what he had meant to me. One day in 1991 I was walking out of the cafeteria and there he was. I hadn't seen the man in thirty years, and there he was, right in front of me, walking down the road toward his car. I called to him, "Mr. Stokes, what are you doing here?" He looked almost the same as I remembered him. He said, "Well, I'm substituting." I took him to our faculty lunchroom and introduced him as the man who was responsible for my becoming a teacher. He seemed pleased by that. We sat and chatted, as we did on two or three more occasions when he subbed at my school.

It isn't often you get to look a teacher in the eyes half a lifetime later and tell him how he influenced your life, but I was blessed enough to do exactly that. I thanked him for his enthusiasm and love of teaching; for the VOICE, the emotion, and the inspiration; and most of all for getting me to think and investigate. He appreciated it and I felt as though something important had been completed. A few years later I heard he had passed away.

KARA KNOTTS
student, teaching credential program

— w r i t i n g   a b o u t —

MRS. CAMUS
her first-grade teacher

EASY AS A, B, C

A . . . B . . . C . . . D. Easy enough, isn't it? But try making a fist with your thumb on top for an *A*, or making a flat palm with your thumb crossed in front for a *B*. Not as easy, is it? I have never been quite clear why my first-grade teacher, Mrs. Camus, taught such a young group of hearing children an abstract idea like sign language. Maybe it was that she had someone in her life who was deaf . . . or maybe she realized each one of us would someday encounter someone who was deaf . . . or maybe she knew the girl on my soccer team was deaf and wanted me to know how to communicate with her. Whatever the reason, Mrs. Camus had a profound impact on my life and I will always thank her for the simple letters and words of wisdom she shared.

To be more precise, the American Sign Language alphabet is

what my first-grade teacher taught us. But she didn't just teach us the alphabet (which we knew by heart within a few short weeks), she also taught us some of the signs for words in the song "Tomorrow" from the musical *Annie*. I can still remember the signs for *tomorrow, sun,* and *love;* if you ask me, there aren't three more important words in *any* language. With these twenty-six letters and basic words, I have kept sign language in my heart for twelve years. Now, finally, I am pursuing a career in deaf education.

When I came to college I was worried I would never find anything I could do for the rest of my life. Mrs. Camus has kindly taken care of that. With the goal of someday being an educator for the deaf or an American Sign Language interpreter, I will never again be at a loss for direction in my life.

MRS. POST'S 6TH-HOUR ENGLISH CLASS

Milwaukee, 1966
Old, white-haired Mrs. Post slippered
her joined and curved 4 fingers into her every
dress' white-laced V-neck. There she

moved her hand metrically up &
down between her freckled breasts
the whole while she read to us.
That day it was Robert Frost.

Reading Frost, by any second
quatrain, Mrs. Post became transported.
Scansion increased her heartbeat.
Spondees visibly shortened her breath.

That hot afternoon we read
"Stopping by Woods on a Snowy
Evening" her recitation
even gave me a slight shiver.

It was summer. Wasps had flown
into our opened classroom windows.
Girls waved hand-folded theme-paper fans;
boys after lunch dozed. The class

had just left the snow-
filled woods on the "darkest evening of the year."
There "the little horse" near the frozen lake
was still shaking his harness bells, &
in the lonely dark the wind was still

blowing. Oh no, now the class was off
to a "yellow wood." Someone was sighing.
It wasn't me. I was lost. I could not keep up,
but I was happily lost in clicking

ice-covered birches, in "magnified apples," in
"domes of heaven." When I finally managed

to catch up, Mrs. Post was in philodendrons.
No, no she wasn't in philodendrons.
She was summing up

"The Road Not Taken": "Phil o soph i cal.
Verrry philosophical." And that was when
she posed the question: "What did Frost mean
'I took the one less traveled by
And that has made all the difference'?"
Now, here, I believe we are close to the moment
where I decide to be a poet. Debbie Siegel,
whose mother—and everyone knows this—
drove the family's mink-colored Impala
into the family swimming pool
only a week before,

Debbie, who everyone knows never speaks
except in gym class or home economics,
raised her arm and
impatiently waved her hand
as if cleaning a stubborn streak off a window.

Possibly in anticipation of all
post-structural theory, Debbie said,
"It is clear
if the speaker of the poem had traveled
the more traveled road, he would
have ended up at the milkman's. Since

he did not need any milk that day,
he took the road less traveled."

What?? Even, even
the most completely uninterested students
perked up then. What was happening?
Mrs. Post's hand flew out of her dress.

Michael Durkin sat up and started sputtering.
Susan O'Toole of the best jumpers and knee socks
was about to try logic. (LOGIC???
What does that have to do with poetry?)
When the bell prizefight-loud rang,

we all returned to our corners, but, & this
is important: We were not untouched.
Judy Feenburg's black ponytail
whipped her cheeks from her agitated
head swinging as she exited.
And I, I believe, I was changed also.
I left Mrs. Post's room bedraggled
with words and their possibilities
to create hallucinations
    quiet breathing
to create bouquets of confusion
    & feasts of loss

and in Debbie Siegel's case that summer afternoon
to focus attention on syntax and grammar.

Never before in Mrs. Post's class,
or in any other class that I shared with her,
had Debbie ever spoken so well

with such precision, such elaborately
constructed and weirdly considered
comments, and I, for one, have always been
grateful to both Debbie and old, white-haired
Mrs. Post, who had the wisdom,
that afternoon, to allow us to leave her
classroom in such sweet suspension of sense,
which I grew to understand as
only one of the many glittered

costumes of the lively breath-
ful poems I am always
growing to love.

Susan Firer
poet, teacher

SONIA DASS
high school senior

— w r i t i n g   a b o u t —

MARILYN HOFFACKER
her eighth-grade history teacher

I remember walking to her class expecting the worst. "Ha-ha," my younger brother had taunted me when I picked up my schedule for eighth grade. The reason: I had Mrs. Marilyn Hoffacker for history. "You're going to have so much homework and project after project in that class," he gloated. Panic gripped me. *Was her class that bad?*

My first impression surprised me, for I saw an essence that contrasted with all the rumors and horror stories I had heard. I met a short, pretty woman with long brown hair; she greeted each of us with a handshake as we walked in.

There was never a dull moment in Mrs. Hoffacker's class, for her carefully planned lessons were always fresh and interesting. Our class did not have book homework, but a combination of group projects, individual writing assignments, videos, and re-creations. We did not just *learn* history, we *relived* it through role-playing and thought-provoking discussions. We founded hypothetical colonies to experience the colonization of early America. Later we learned about slavery and the Civil War through holding a simulated slave auction, and writing our own war journals based on video notes. It was as if history had seduced me, and the intellectual affair was fulfilling. It became one of my favorite classes, so much so that while I failed tests in algebra, I excelled in history.

Though easygoing, Mrs. Hoffacker didn't put up with any back-talk; she could stare us into silence any time. Though short, she seemed to tower over even the toughest bully and make him cringe. It was no big deal to make other teachers mad—in fact, we relished the idea—but we knew not to annoy Mrs. Hoffacker. At the same time, she was fun. I recall one time during the spring she was shooting passersby from her window with a toy water gun.

Mrs. Hoffacker was not just a great teacher, but a good friend as well. She was my confidante; I remember many afternoons talking with her. Not many teachers can do that—be a rigorous academic teacher and also a compassionate friend willing to extend a heart to some bewildered adolescent needing solace. She was a medium through which I could understand the adult world in my chaotic coming of age. Perhaps because she had her own teenager, she understood our needs and emotions. Mrs. Hoffacker was like a mother to me; she always knew when I was feeling down and was always ready and willing to give me a comforting hug.

In a few months, I will graduate from high school and embark on a journey toward a rewarding career. After much thought, I have decided to become a teacher—not just any teacher, but a Marilyn Hoffacker. I know this is impossible, for I am not her, but I *can* strive to capture her essence and continue her legacy. I want to have the same impact on others that she had on me. I want to be a teacher who not only teaches the facts, but also provides guidance and support. Many kids go astray because they think no one cares; I want to be there for my students and lead them to the right path.

Marilyn Hoffacker taught me about history, but she also taught me how to love and respect myself and others. Her class was tough, yet it was worth every hour studying late into the night. I remember the last day of school when she gave her lecture about life. She ended her emotional speech with ". . . and if you guys ever need me, I'm in the phone book."

As a senior swirling in stress, I often take a minute and close my eyes; I think of when I was 14, listening to Mrs. Hoffacker lecture. Yes, I learned my history, but I also learned not to let this world grind me down. Thanks, Mrs. Hoffacker.

ELAYNE CLIFT
writer, teacher

—— w r i t i n g a b o u t ——

ESTHER PETERSON
her friend and mentor

MY ELEANOR: A TRIBUTE TO ESTHER PETERSON

I first met Esther during the final days of the Carter administration. A group of women activists were meeting at the White House about the dumping of unapproved consumer goods in the Third World. Esther said, "You can count on me. I can't offer much, but I have a big dining room table, and we'll just work there if we have to."

Shortly after that I wrote a profile article about her. During the interview I heard about her Utah childhood, her foray into the labor movement, and her AFL–CIO stint as a lobbyist. Long after the profile had been published, our connection was strengthened whenever our paths crossed at meetings and ceremonies. Her greeting and interest in my work warmed me against the chill of such Washington occasions. Esther was one of those people who made you feel you were the only one in the room when she spoke to you.

Gradually I began to call upon her for advice and information, and soon we were in regular contact. That is how I became part of a group fostered by Esther and several others to preserve Val Kil, Eleanor Roosevelt's beloved home in Hyde Park, New York.

When I visited the estate, I saw the furniture, the mementos, and the private space that had nourished Mrs. Roosevelt. I read this extraordinary woman's biography. I watched Maureen Stapleton portray an Eleanor who asked of women to find their "souls of iron." At last I understood why Esther loved and admired Eleanor, with whom she had worked.

Esther began her career in Boston, where she taught the daughters of wealthy businessmen. At night she tutored a different set of girls: factory workers' daughters who often supplemented their family's income by doing piecework at home. One night the young women told Esther they were planning to strike. Afer they had left, Esther wondered what it was about. "Go and find out," her husband urged. She did: The girls had been sewing square pockets on aprons. When the manufacturer wanted them done in the shape of hearts, it took longer, so the girls could not earn as much per hour. Unwilling to stand by and witness this injustice, Esther ended up leading and winning what became known as the Heart Breakers Strike.

When she and Oliver moved to Washington, D.C., where he was to serve in government, she saw an opportunity to advocate with greater impact. Esther quickly became involved in the labor movement on a national scale. Inevitably, plenty of opposition followed the first woman lobbyist for the AFL–CIO. But she did not stop with labor advocacy.

When Esther tried to establish an Office of Consumer Representation, Congress defeated the bill. She condemned big business for using distortions, scare tactics, and even outright lies to influence Congress. No wonder her admirers called her "the grande dame of the consumer movement" while political cartoonists labeled her "the most dangerous thing since Genghis Khan" and "a global nanny."

"What are we going to do with Esther?" one man had asked when she was assigned to a senator to lobby on behalf of the AFL–CIO. "Oh, give her to Kennedy," another replied. "He won't amount to anything!" And that is how Esther Peterson, who had become his friend, became Director of the Women's Bureau under President John F. Kennedy. She served President Johnson as Assistant Secretary of Labor, and President Jimmy Carter as Special Assistant for Consumer Affairs. In her later years, Esther worked with the International Union of Labor Organizations and served as a representative to the United Nations at the request of President Bill Clinton.

Ever the activist and advocate, she moved mountains when it came to women, labor issues, and consumer rights. But Esther was also a woman in love with her husband, a mother devoted to her four children, and a marvelous friend and mentor to me.

I remember one day in particular. I went to her home to interview her for a book I was researching. We settled in to talk about her early life and her subsequent political role. I started out posing interview questions, but they soon led us down a path of personal conversation that moved, amused, and inspired me. There seemed no age gap between us; we were simply two women connecting, and telling the truth about our lives.

When we were ready for lunch, a frail but determined Esther took my arm, and said in a whisper, "I'm so pleased to be going out; today is my 64th wedding anniversary." I felt especially moved to be sharing the day with her because I knew how deeply she loved her Oliver (who had died some years before).

At lunch we toasted him, she reminisced, and then we spoke of many things: love and marriage and even sex. We raved about politics, always ending a topic in violent agreement. We remembered our lost sisters, and we spoke of death and grief and sibling rivalry. We fantasized about journeying together on the Orient Express or on a banana boat in Brazil. We spoke of friendship and poetry, of the quality of life and of the demise of civilization. In those moments, I felt so exalted by this great woman's friendship that I dared not wait to tell her what I had been feeling for a long time.

"I want you to know something," I said, trying to contain the vast emotion I felt. "I want you to know you are my Eleanor."

"Oh, my dear," she replied, her eyes welling with tears. "If only you truly knew me, you would never say that!" Then, grasping my hands in hers, Esther said simply, "Thank you. Thank you . . . you know what that means to me, don't you?"

We saw a good deal of each other after that, sharing meals, museums, or cups of tea in her sitting room. Esther came regularly to my home for Seder, grew fond of my family, and included us in her 90th-birthday celebration. When she was inducted into the National Women's Hall of Fame, I was there. But for me, no occasion or celebration was quite so special as the day I confessed my admiration—and she accepted it with such grace.

PATTERNS

Mrs. Irwin walked up and down the aisles reciting
Amy Lowell's poem "Patterns."

She took measured steps
as she passed our desks . . .

up and down   up and down

There was something in her voice
that made me think of a candle flame
flickering in red glass
in the corner of a dark cathedral.

You could tell she had left our classroom
to walk in Amy's Lady's garden

among the squills and daffodils . . .
You could tell she felt the stays
of that whalebone corset,
the train of that "stiff,
brocaded gown"
trailing behind her
over the garden path.

From her trembling voice you knew
she felt those waistcoat buttons
pressing into her flesh.

The next day Mrs. Irwin took us to visit
Mr. Eliot's cellar. We heard the rats' feet scurrying
over the broken glass.
It was heady stuff for the '50s,
for our little northern California town
surrounded by the moat
of those Eisenhower years.
We didn't know what to make of Mrs. Irwin,
who pulled her black hair
back into a bun
and wore a smooth stone
on a leather thong around her neck.
We didn't know what to make of Mrs. Irwin's
sandals and socks below a skirt
hanging a little too long.

If you use your imagination—if you have a similar
memory buried—perhaps you can visualize
how we treated Mrs. Irwin and her passion.

What could I tell her
if I met her now?

I see her somber face, the little stone
she wore around her neck,
her measured steps
as she walked up and down
the aisles of our classroom—
"Amy's Lady" and all those poems
pulsing through her mind and heart,

her voice
resonating
even
now
Patterns?

I think of her life
crossing mine.

If I could tell her, I would tell her that.

                          Diane Southwick Granger

Amy Friedman Fraser
writer, college writing teacher

— w r i t i n g   a b o u t —

Donald Barthelme
her writing teacher

Remembering the Teachings of Don B

"You should have seen Tenth Street when it was The Village," I wanted to say when I introduced my students to his writings and they stared at me blankly.

I stared back but was thinking of a day more than twenty years earlier when I first walked nervously across Tenth Street toward Don B's house and stepped into the great man's living room. Don B would chuckle to hear me call him great because he was a chuckler, someone who looked at the whole world—including all those known as great—with a wary eye, an eye for the absurd and the true. He would have turned my characterization of him as "great" into something else again, something written in crystalline, bohemian, bonkers, ball-busting prose. He would have penned a hilariously sad story about a former student—gone grey and halfway to seed—returning to an old haunt, now a beyond-the-hip place, to visit a man she called great. He would have had a grand time with such a story, and with such a characterization of himself.

That first afternoon in September 1978, it was humid outside, though I don't remember ever feeling anything but a comfortable, close humidity in Barthelme's presence. Something about him—the slight Texan drawl, the incomparable beard, the boots, the jeans, the thin-lipped smile, the narrow, blue-eyes-behind-tiny-gold-framed-glasses stare. The gentle way he pushed toward honesty, and straight-shooting, pure prose, the way every comma had to be in the right place (oh God, are they?)—all that made every moment with him like one of those late summer days when the whole world is blooming and humid, and a storm is moving in, and you want to sing about hot rods and backseat love and hot sauce and gods. Something about Don B made my mind always simmer or broil.

Some critics call him cool. I can think of no one less cool, though he was hip in his way, and in this politically correct era he might have been considered incorrect. I remember once someone said, and it just might have been him, that a man who marries four times, as he did, is the ultimate optimist. Yes, I think Don B *was* that, in a melancholy Texan way.

Thomas Pynchon, one of the handful of writers who could do justice to a biography of Don B, called him "notoriously uncategorizable." Lisa Zeidner, a former colleague, once wrote she wished he were still around to allude to the O.J. freeway chase; as Zeidner put it, "Even the phrase 'white bronco,' with its crisp consonants, seems somehow Don B–like." This media-blitzed, whacked-out world could use DB's cool, clear, funny, philosophical, woefully joyful voice.

Don B met with us City College students in his home, which he no doubt did in part because it was easier than traveling up to Harlem to teach, easier to cope with this slew of hungry-for-praise-and-publication students on his own turf. And it is equally likely that he welcomed us to his home because that was a familiar down-home custom he'd inherited from his down-home Texan roots.

Barthelme was the love of my life as a writer. I entered the graduate program at City College of New York because he taught there. And then there I was, in his living room on Tenth Street across the street from Grace Paley, another of the greats. That was when the village was The Village.

Don B took each of us—male, female, young, old, lame, degenerate—into his home and took each of us seriously. He read our work, poised his pen, and took aim, offering professional, respectful, hard-driving editorial advice while remaining friendly, sexy, and dear. He did that tightrope act as surely as he did the tightrope act that is his writing.

He was the most assured and stringent editor I've ever known, and he was great in a cool, WASPy, Texan, country-and-western, sophisticated New York way. He was, like the things he loved, a collage, impossible to stereotype or frame. Underneath, I always felt, he was a heartfelt sap, and his stories always had that edge—the irony that is not quite irony because, suddenly, he'll land a deep-down-to-the-bone sad moment, and then he'll zap you a moment later with curl-your-toes joy.

I am still in love with Don B but not in the schoolgirl-crush way. I simply want, always, to write something Don B would love. When in 1989 he died of throat cancer, suddenly and surprisingly to those of us who had moved on, I felt I'd let him down. I had just signed a contract for my first book that came out months after he passed away. For ten years I had planned to send Don B the first copy of my first book. He was the person I most wanted to thank.

I hadn't, as I told a friend, "made it." Hadn't had a hit. But I know he didn't exactly believe in hits. He knew when a sentence hit paydirt, and when one crashed. He knew good. He knew truth. He would be chuckling like crazy by now at the notion of being placed on such a lofty pedestal. He would attach a balloon to that pedestal and somewhere in the midst of this impromptu story someone would pop the balloon. I'm not sure where he would land, but I know the journey would send everyone reeling and thinking and feeling.

Out of our class of twelve came a writing group that lasted six years and friends who have remained close for twenty. Don B seemed in those days to be the calm, thoughtful center in the midst of the flashy, the famous, the fiery. Our other teachers—famous, fabulous, fine writers—were often at war in some way or another. Seeing Don B, listening to him, talking to him, felt as comfortable as a long, slow fishing trip; and sometimes we caught something. He spoke admiringly of his fellow famous and like-minded writers—Coover, Gass, Barth, Hawkes—the so-called postmodernists who knew how to write, to think, to entertain, to delight, to disarm.

He seemed a little sad in the early '80s. He drank too much and smoked too many cigarettes. He was wry and could be a harsh social critic, and never apologetic about that. And he was wonderful to troubled young people. One of those troubled young men in our class one day stole some books from Don B's bookshelves. The next week this young man brought in a story he'd written about a fellow who steals books from a famous writer's shelves. DB worked with him on that story, ultimately helping the young man to rework the ending—which involved the return of the books. It was a marvelous metaphor to watch.

So twenty years later—nearly ten since he so suddenly died—I handed out copies of *Me and Miss Mandible* to my own group of hungry-for-praise-and-publication students. When I asked them what they thought, they were silent. I wanted to say to those students before me, "This is what writing can be, but none of us will ever write like this. His writing is what today's newscasters might call 'very unique.' And he would have a field day with such an oxymoronic phrase."

I couldn't tell my students their not "getting" the story made me even more sad than the fact that he was gone. I couldn't telephone and say, "Don B, I need your teachings. What do I tell people who read a story so melancholy and so funny and so pointed and so right-on-the-mark as your *Miss Mandible*, when they look up and their eyes go white as a dead chicken's. Worse, what do I say when I ask them to read another Barthelme story, but they want to talk about the *Titanic*.

I can imagine the fun DB would have had with the *Titanic* mania, and so I don't weep in front of my students; instead I begin quietly to chuckle.

I look out at the sea of blank faces and veer toward tragedy, and then I remember Don B never permitted the easy swoon toward tragedy. He had no patience for the cheap, the mechanical, the easy. This is why, whenever I try to teach students *about* his stories, I come away breathless, wordless. Everything I say sounds too easy. Like calling DB "great."

When I think of the teachings of Don B, I think of the man who knew that life can be dull, but art sings. And making art of life is one way to ensure that life is more than life . . . that sometimes, on good, humid, stormy days, life can be almost as delicious as art, that the two might be one.

SITTING BEHIND ROBERT BLY AT THE PALACE OF FINE ARTS

As I sat behind you in the auditorium,
I had this urge to reach out
and massage your magnificent white scalp.
My own father's head being bald and greasy,
I occasionally massaged his Humpty-Dumpty head
while he sat in his huge recliner chair.
But your hair sat on your head
like a whirl of San Francisco fog,
like a halo of Minnesota snow
so thick and beautiful.
I wanted to touch its roots,
feel your delicate thoughts surface
humming inside your skull.
I wanted my fingers to circle each of your temples
and bow before them.

Who are the guardians of your gate,
oh, Captain,
and who are the guardians of mine?

Last night I dreamed of a mansion.
There were so many rooms,
and I could choose any one I wanted to sleep in.
I want to sleep inside your skull.
I want to read you like Braille,
hearing no sounds coming up from your gut,
just pure thought rising,
singing at the base of each hair follicle
while my fingertips pick up
these tiny Morse code messages
and through osmosis my body knows
what the guardians of the gate keep secret.

Terri Glass
poet, teacher

ROBERT SCHNELLE
college teacher

— w r i t i n g a b o u t —

"MOSHER"
his English professor

A SOURCE, A BRINGER OF THE WORD

We create our heroes; we are created by them. The mind, that vessel and busy editor, has ensured the lineage of paragons from Achilles to Chuck Yeager, from Sacajawea to JFK. Who cares that Socrates was a lecher and Mickey Mantle a lush? Youth must test its mettle in the glow of ideals made flesh. If Dennis Rodman looks tarnished by the memory of DiMaggio, give him time. Reports of the hero's demise are hasty.

As I waded through adolescence in a dearth of Olympian influences, I was luckier than most. There were many who taught us competently at the New Hampshire boarding school I attended. In addition to its family men and wool-gathering bachelors, the academy even managed to employ a few masters with genuine panache—virile athletes and sports car aficionados, men's men in a world of boys. But I didn't cotton to these fellows; they and their admirers exuded a certain bonding oil I lacked. The teacher I now think most of appeared to me then a mere kindly geezer, as unremarkable as the tone of the bell in Baxter Hall tower.

Mosher was his name. He carried himself like a terrapin in tweeds, and he could often be seen walking the road that led from his quarters in Brewster House along through a tunnel of sugar maples, across a covered bridge, and up the long hill that crested at the heart of the campus. Nearsighted, he wore "fleshies" on the bridge of his nose, and he parted his hair just left of center, twenties style. Mosher did not smoke a pipe.

Yet every morning he talked about words, poems, and sentences in the outmoded science lab that served as our English classroom. It was there among butterfly collections that I memorized "The Need of Being Versed in Country Things"; it was there, too, that I heard an aging gentleman explain why, when out walking, he always greeted passing strangers on the road.

Enunciating gently through a Down-East brogue, Mosher gave words an epigrammatic quality. He lectured at greater length than is now fashionable in classrooms, but he never droned, preferring to punctuate his syllables with choice pauses and articulations of a single, hoary eyebrow. Why is it, then, that I recall so little of what Mosher actually said? Instead I remember the way he listened, nodding and murmuring, "Yes, hmmm . . . Oh, indeed?" while my roommate, vice president of our class, detailed his personal method of writing prose in a trance.

There were the weeks when Mosher tolerated my dozing through senior seminar, finally taking me aside one day to inquire about my health. The lives of his students were acknowledged but not intruded on. Perhaps, after all, he knew the limits of his influence. Like many good teachers, Mosher conveyed his influence through gestures. Still, it was words he valued publicly.

My dog-eared copy of Mosher's graduation address begins, "I have nothing to give you but words." The body of Mosher's speech must have escaped me all those years ago; I read it now as if listening for the first time. Yet his closing image revives a weird flush of gratitude. He compares his students to birds, and he tells us to "be good, be true, fly high, fly wherever your lives may take you." He would have been appalled by recent literary theory, for I believe he loved above all the music of language and its power to bond people to some Platonic ideal.

Unconsciously heroic, Mosher was a messenger, a bearer of the word. As the prodigy is evolution's wild card, teaching the rest of us to whittle flutes from kindling or fashion forges with sticks of fire, the messenger is humanity's mentor. His gifts may not derive from genius, but without them we'd have no map, no words to hold experience. Mosher brought the word to hundreds of young wanderers, and through him I found a vocation.

Far from the valley where Mosher released his fledglings, I earn my living teaching English at a chronically underfunded state college. Unlike Mosher, I serve the children of agribusinessmen and convenience store owners, young people whose concern for the eternal verities is, putting it gently, unrealized. Still, at their best, the classroom's purposes justify a profession that doesn't pay in any worldly sense. I tell myself that each fifty-minute burst is a chance to redeem American youth from relativism, or at least to play cat and mouse with freshmen who grow ever younger and less conversant with words.

Just as often, unfortunately, I wonder what Mosher would say to the girl in the back row of my Composition 102 class, spine slumped to the wall, eyes a pair of burned-out vacuum tubes, tee shirt baldly declaring, "Fuck This Shit." How would he respond to an incompetent Introduction to Literature essay denouncing Shakespeare's works as "racist, Eurocentric trash"?

Uneasy lies the head that wears a baseball cap, say I. When the teaching goes well, I think of Mosher. But when it falters, as it often does, I remember him, too. This is not a Mr. Chips tale, Mosher being too skeptical and elusive to play the role of a sentimental codger. Yet he was an old man when I found him, long past his years of dormitory and coaching obligations—perhaps others knew another Mosher. One thing was sure, he had been acquainted with melancholy.

During the early seventies, those freewheeling days of the student elective, we who enrolled in his courses term after term learned to gloss our teacher. "Old Mosh is bumming today," somebody would remark, a signal to the rest of us to tread lightly as we entered class. Not that Mosher ever scorned or bullied his students. On these occasions he might have been an actor in a Beckett play, his audience puzzling in the shadows, each side intimate but inscrutable to the other.

In black moods Mosher soliloquized. "I know few things for certain," he once averred. "But if you think the world you live in now resembles the world you are going to live in, you're kidding yourself." He spoke of effort and of obstacles to achievement. He talked of the writing life, and he disparaged his own talents as a wordsmith.

Long before, he had earned wages composing text for a soap opera comic strip while struggling with an unpublishable novel.

Intoning the tragic muse as he did, our teacher could make us write. We sensed that we, too, might fall short of our desire. Of course, teachers who choose their profession out of love for the printed word are like prison guards enthralled by masonry. I'm sure Mosher understood this. Sooner or later, the word love that draws English teachers to an institutioned life becomes a goad, and the crude humanity we are charged with seems all the more a letdown for that once-entrancing vision.

Mosher, however, had done Bohemia. Writing failed to support him, so he taught. If Mosher carried resentment, only concern for his students betrayed him, for experience barbed his sympathy. Mosher's generosity lay in this: Come of age in an era when schoolteachers assumed omniscience, he stood before us as a mortal. And yet, modesty wouldn't have mattered had Mosher been incompetent. On the contrary, he valued duty, he understood his role, and he taught like a master.

Perhaps Mosher followed his favorite poet's advice. In a letter to a friend, Robert Frost once declared that "life was a risk I had to take and took." Whatever stoic false limbs Mosher leaned on, he worked effectively. He instituted a then-revolutionary practice by having his students write responses to each other's work. We kept interpretive notebooks. We staged scenes from plays we read, and we wrote fanciful character biographies. Composition and literature were not presented as recondite subjects, and they had not yet become a forum for nihilistic word games and victim competition. Higher knowledge was understood to be fathomable to those who honed their skills, and in Mosher's class we honed them daily. When he wrote at the top of my essay, "This moves me along," I sensed that teachers can be an audience you might want to deserve.

Once, on his way down the long country road that crossed a covered bridge before it climbed again, Mosher paused to speak with a student. Any boarding school teacher would recognize the type—bewildered, self-absorbed, ashamed of being a scholarship kid in Goodwill tailoring, and just at that moment AWOL from afternoon sports. The elder asked the younger to walk with him. As they went along, he identified the songs of the hermit thrush and red-eyed vireo. He said he had liked the student's composition about Mr. Frost's "Ovenbird" and he pointed to a beech grove where he had seen the creature of that name. Teacher and student walked a mile more. At last, before parting, Mosher said something about the power of affinities; I wish I could remember his words. Their content rested in the tact of the man's gaze as he looked off toward Mount Ascutney, in the dignity he afforded his listener.

Mosher, you've been gone for years. How many lacked the good grace to thank you? Belatedly, I claim you as my teacher, a hero and bringer of news. I can say that your story ends happily because the news you brought has stayed news. But my debt to you I settle as you must have settled your own, gathering conviction in the heart, carrying on with the living.

CHAPTER 8

THE TORCHBEARERS

*Tributes from students to teachers—
followed by the teachers' tributes
to their teachers.*

Education is simply the soul of a society as it
passes from one generation to another.

—*G. K. Chesterton*

Roy Shaffin
rabbinical school student

— w r i t i n g   a b o u t —

Jack DeRieux
his high school drama teacher

As a student at the University of Judaism, I learned that the word *rabbi* is not only defined as someone who has earned rabbinic ordination; it is also another word for teacher. Mr. DeRieux was my teacher for Drama and Production Workshop during my four years at Northgate High School in Walnut Creek, California. One day, I extended Mr. DeRieux a surprise visit. I entered the classroom and said, "Shalom, rabbi." Mr. DeRieux does not have rabbinic ordination. He is not even Jewish. But to me, Mr. DeRieux exemplifies the virtues and character of the great Jewish sages.

In his class, there was something more desirable than a good grade: Mr. DeRieux's eyes glimmering with pride when you performed well. Disappointment on his face was something all of us tried to prevent at all costs. Mr. DeRieux used his acting skill to influence us: Through facial expression, he inspired his students to excel; I do not remember him ever raising his voice at a student.

Mr. DeRieux instilled in his students an insatiable love for the theater. He taught a philosophy called method acting where the objective of the actor is to know and become the character. When I was involved in *The Diary of Anne Frank,* Mr. DeRieux asked the actors to spend 24 hours on the set—and remain in character. Afraid of disturbing people in the offices below, we remained quiet during the day. But when night came, we returned to the pleasantries of family life, releasing our thoughts, desires, and complaints in normal speaking voices. We simulated the conditions our characters had endured in hiding during the Holocaust. This exercise taught us the extent to which an actor must sometimes go to really know a character.

Mr. DeRieux would coax us to extend our boundaries by saying, "I would encourage you to . . ." or "I would suggest that you try . . ." He would complete this advice with words that inspired a student to try something new. He would ask some to take a small step, others, a huge leap. Other times Mr. DeRieux's words were so meaningful they gave students a new perspective on their character, their scenes, drama, and sometimes life itself. He encouraged us to reach beyond our preconceived boundaries and barriers and learn what it means to be an actor.

Mr. DeRieux was not only an incredible teacher, but also a role model. He cared less about what style of clothing a person wore and more about what was inside. In a society dominated by the propaganda of Guess?, Calvin Klein, and Reebok, he tried to bring out the best from within people. He was also not afraid to stand up for an unpopular opinion. One day the issue of condom distribution came up in one of his classes. Knowing his opinion would be unpopular, Mr. DeRieux nevertheless expressed his thoughts about the sanctity of sex. He explained to his students that he believed they were too young to be involved in sexual activity.

Oftentimes when students graduate, they lose contact with

their teachers. Mr. DeRieux, however, remains a significant force in my life. I still visit him often. I trust him with delicate matters in my life and I listen closely to what he has to say.

Although it has been a while since I performed, not long ago I auditioned for a play. Before I walked onstage, I envisioned Mr. DeRieux standing before me. During this mystical experience, Mr. DeRieux's words and teachings came back as if I had never left high school. They often help me with public speaking, delivering presentations, and conveying my ideas. Mr. DeRieux is still my teacher really.

He continues to show me how to live, as well as how to perform. Once, I came back to Northgate High to see a Production Workshop play. I was again impressed when I saw Mr. DeRieux setting up tables, chairs, coffee, and refreshments before the play began. Mr. DeRieux is a man of stature and prestige; but he is also a man of humility. He was not at all embarrassed to perform such a menial task. On the contrary, Mr. DeRieux was proud to make yet another contribution to the success of his students and the show. This incident reminded me of when I was one of the scenery crew: Mr. DeRieux got down on his hands and knees and sawed and painted with us; he was never too proud to do the dirty work. He had not changed.

I try to emulate his humility. Mr. DeRieux never said, "I am honored." Instead he said, "I am humbled." When I became a Hebrew school teacher, I employed many of his techniques: I heard myself saying phrases such as "I would encourage you to . . ." and "I would suggest that you try . . ." And I never yelled or spoke disrespectfully to my students.

About a year ago, Mr. DeRieux was in a car accident. He was seriously injured and in pain for a long time. He was physically limited. The first time I saw him after the accident, he was struggling to do things he easily could have done before. Many people would have just given up and allowed their bodies to sink into old age. But Mr. DeRieux was determined to revive his abilities so he could continue to contribute to his students and live his life to the fullest.

Through intense physical therapy and incredible dedication, he restored his health. The next time I went to visit him, he was just as physically fit and vibrant as he had been before the accident. Mr. DeRieux is a role model of not giving up, of continuing to strive even in the darkest of times. His example has provided me with inspiration to persevere and to overcome my fears.

Shakespeare wrote, "All the world's a stage, and all the men and women merely players." Mr. DeRieux taught me that all the awareness of surroundings, emotions, and people an actor cultivates for the stage can be applied to life too. He showed me each of us has a choice: You can live life as an old black-and-white script in antiquated English, or you can bring this play to life by transforming the world into a grand stage.

— w r i t i n g   a b o u t —

MILO PRICE
his eleventh-grade speech teacher

I remember watching Mr. Price on campus prior to taking his class: His struggle getting from one location to another was inspirational; he needed the support of two canes when walking. The students did not know what caused his disability, but among teenagers there was plenty of speculation.

I cannot remember why I enrolled in Mr. Price's speech class my junior year of high school. In that period of my life I was painfully shy. When asked to speak, I would get embarrassed and blush beet red. I had not yet found my voice.

Mr. Price often sat on a wooden stool in front of the class; it allowed him to rest while listening to students' presentations. When he wanted to write something on the chalkboard, he pulled himself up to a standing position and with the assistance of his canes, shuffled to the board. He hung one cane on the chalk tray as he wrote down important points.

After listening to our speeches, he commented aloud, then returned our papers with written suggestions. For the first time in high school I received strongly positive evaluations; Mr. Price let me know how much he enjoyed my work. Because of these affirmative responses I worked harder; I wanted to live up to his image of me. One day Mr. Price told me I "had been given a gift." *A gift? Me?* He explained, "You have a great speaking voice, Jack." I was dumbfounded.

I began to feel more and more comfortable with every speech. I actually began looking forward to each new assignment. What a miracle! From the painfully shy teenager who used to turn red in front of any audience, I became a confident young man who had found his voice. I began to enjoy public speaking.

On the last day of class Mr. Price said something that startled me: "Jack, I think you could do very well in drama. You should take our drama class." *Could he be talking to me? Actually getting up in front of an audience and performing?*

I followed Mr. Price's advice and the following year I enrolled in drama. I felt the approval of my peers when I successfully performed in a children's play, and later in the year played the lead role in our school musical. I savored my newfound success. My senior year became an extraordinary time for me.

The following year I registered in a junior college and enrolled in drama, where I continued to develop my talent. I graduated from San Francisco State University with a major in Theatre Arts. Drama has supported me as a teacher and I have continued to act in the Bay Area theatre community for the past thirty years.

I thank you, Milo Price, for your introduction and encouragement into the wonderful world of theatre—one I would never have found without your care and intervention. You helped a young man discover his voice and that discovery led to a vision of his place in this life.

JOSHUA DiBIANCA
telecommunications project manager

— w r i t i n g a b o u t —

DICK FRISS
his twelfth-grade English teacher

My favorite teacher, Dick Friss, taught English, but English was merely the vehicle he used to arouse his students. In Mr. Friss' class, teens were awakened from their deep slumber and encouraged to taste, feel, and hear life breathing within and around them. It was in Mr. Friss' class that I met Holden Caufield. With Mr. Friss' guidance and Holden Caufield in the background, I learned the importance of being true to myself.

I recall one time I had to leave class early to catch a bus because I was on the baseball team. "Mr. Friss," I asked, "is it all right if I leave?"

"I don't know, Josh," Mr. Friss replied. "What do you think?" This exchange epitomized Mr. Friss' legacy. He never gave the answer; he always forced students to find their own answers. He built individuals' sense of self by creating a classroom climate that inspired introspection. Every day we would ask Mr. Friss questions and every day he would turn the questions around and direct them right back in our faces.

Mr. Friss could see through any superficial comments I said or writings I submitted. He urged me to dig deeper into my soul to articulate my visions, feelings, and desires. He encouraged me to think independently—without relying on the comfort of my family or friends for support. I was naked for the first time and the only savior was myself.

Now, as I enter the working world, so many of the tasks I perform have standard operating procedures. Standard operating procedures stifle creativity and innovation. Sadly, many colleagues I work with have accepted these automated tasks as reality. When a situation occurs that does not fit into a common procedure, they are baffled: Where do they find the answer? Somewhere along the line they have relinquished the power of looking from within.

The business world rewards individuals who are innovative and who dare to try new approaches. I recently was promoted in my first job and the manager I work under explained to me that she liked my ability to "think outside the box." I liked the sound of that.

"Thinking outside the box." A Mr. Friss specialty.

Mr. Friss was a teacher, psychologist, mentor, and friend. I was a 15-year-old boy when I entered Mr. Friss' class. I left it a 16-year-old man.

DICK FRISS
retired teacher

—— w r i t i n g   a b o u t ——

JACK SHEEDY
his college English teacher

I had saved a required course called Principles of Literary Form for my senior year of college. From faculty and fellow students, I'd heard it was the hardest, most demanding course in terms of thought, creativity, and number of papers to be written. Looking through the course catalogue, I saw two names. One was an instructor I'd had for Psychology in Literature the year before. He was an easygoing man whose background in his subject was adequate, but I felt I had learned all I could from him. Besides, if I took his class, I could predict what each day would be like; what I really wanted was a challenge. The other name listed for the course I was about to take was "Sheedy." I'd never heard of him. The unknown might provide the challenge I desired, but still I hesitated and asked around.

"Take Fineberg. It's an easy A for you."

"What's to learn, except where the best ski slopes and bunnies are?"

"Well, if you really want to work your ass off, but learn from a fantastic teacher, take Sheedy."

"Sheedy? Are you kidding? That guy thinks all we've got to do with our lives is write his papers. He's weird."

Well, I couldn't resist. I "took" Sheedy, but by the end of the second week I felt like I'd been taken. I was snowed under with work and bombarded from all sides by ever-changing ways of examining a piece of literature. The idea of symbolic structure in a poem, play, or novel was difficult to perceive, something like a hologram. You could examine a segment of a good piece of writing and in its structure see the structure of the whole.

Another weird thing about this man was he required us to submit rough drafts of major papers two weeks before the final paper was due. It seemed like extra work. I later learned he did this so he could help us; if we were taking an unfruitful direction, he could turn us around and we would still have time to revise or begin anew. Even when my writing was not so hot—a C paper—he commented endlessly regarding what was good about it, and made suggestions for improvement. Often I found myself up at night, writing and rewriting, hating this extensive invasion of my already diminished time, but loving those moments when I succeeded, when I surprised myself with my own intellectual analysis and writing skill.

Further evidence of his weirdness was that in an academic system where instructors had to have a doctorate, he had only a master's degree. How did he get away with it and get rehired each year? He was an extensively published writer! Learning this, my admiration soared. He was actually doing what he was trying to teach us: writing and succeeding.

By the end of the semester, after a month of reading, research, conferences, writing, and rewriting, I handed in a typed, twenty-page paper on the symbolic structure of Ibsen's *Hedda Gabler*. This was my final piece of writing for the course. I was satisfied

I had done my best, but, more than that, I wanted it to be something Sheedy would like to read.

The week before the papers were returned was sheer hell. I tried to lose myself in work for other courses, but instead found myself wondering if Sheedy had read my paper. In class I tried to read some reaction on his face: nothing. Then came the day when the papers were returned. With trepidation I opened the cover, saw a clean title page, and began to read through: no comments. Then, at the bottom of the last page, in his usual precise handwriting, was the line: "An excellent job: This is, I believe, the best of the papers produced from this class."

In that one semester with Jack Sheedy, sixteen years ago, I learned that writing is a demanding mistress. Now, as then, he serves as a model writer and teacher. By his actions he taught me that "if you're going to be a maverick in a conventional world, you'd better be damn good; then and only then, will you be allowed to do what you do best." In working tirelessly and patiently with me, he gave me a part of myself I'd not known before—the writer. But above all, he led me to an understanding of symbolic structure in all of life, helping me make sense of an often senseless universe.

FRANK ALLOCCO, JR
student

— w r i t i n g   a b o u t —

FRANK ALLOCCO
his father and basketball coach

The coach and mentor who influenced me most was my father. When I played for him, I learned a lot more than just how to play basketball: He stressed loyalty, love for my team-mates, and ways to succeed in life. As a coach, these were his legacies.

The most important concept he showed us was, you can't turn a switch on and off: If you are going to be a winner on the court, you have to be a winner off the court. Being good kids, being respectful to adults and our parents, and not causing trouble at school were just as important as showing up on time for practice and working our butts off on the court. My dad upheld this concept steadfastly.

He had a strict rule about team members' dressing for every game in a tie, dress pants, and the school's red sweater. His first year on the job at Northgate, I remember his best scorer was averaging 17 points a game. One night this player showed up in jeans. My dad said, "You can't play tonight unless you go home and change your pants." The kid hurried home—and still missed the first half of the game. Many coaches would have let the guy slide because he was the team's star player. My dad wouldn't bend the rules for anyone. In fact, two weeks later he kicked that same guy off the team for swearing too much and getting in trouble around school. I admire my father for applying the same standards to everyone.

He really felt strongly it was important for us to live right—not just play basketball well. He wanted his players to do the right thing, both on and off the court. What he meant by this was expressed in a story he told us just before an important game early in the season of my junior year. Many years before, he had been playing tennis one day. A pond with ducks was outside the court. While he was playing, he noticed a guy and his dog arrive at the pond; the dog began chasing the ducks and biting them. My dad left the court and yelled at the guy, who collected his dog and left. The ducks were safe. It was an example of someone taking a risk to do the right thing.

"Taking care of the ducks" became our slogan that year. Soon we began taking pride in being the team that did the right thing. Before every game—particularly those against teams known to play rough or violate restrictions on recruiting—we'd repeat, "Okay, let's go take care of the ducks!"

Taking care of the ducks involved a lot, but five things really stick out for me: respect, pride, loyalty, concentration, and teamwork. Dad always told us to respect all opponents, but to fear none. We carried this attitude into every game. We wanted to win with dignity, and to play the game of basketball without taking cheap shots at people or talking a lot of trash. There was plenty of trash talk out there, but it never started with a Northgate player. He made us believe talking trash took our concentration away from the task at hand. If we were worrying about what we were going to say after a shot, then our heads weren't in the game. Basketball requires 100% concentration, and you lose it if you're thinking about the refs, the fans, the other coach, or the opposing players.

Concentration also applied to loyalty and teamwork. We wanted to play our best so we didn't let the other guys down. This started off the court as loyalty to friends and carried onto the floor as loyalty to four other players. And we worked hard. A lot of high school coaches run practices that resemble scrimmages on a playground: lots of shooting. All our practices were geared to defense—at least an hour of defense every afternoon. There were players that didn't fit into the Northgate system of teamwork and defense, but they either changed or quit. On our locker room wall was a sign: "This program is not for everyone, but those who stay will be champions."

Because of his system and our hard work, we did become state champions. And we won with a team that, talent-wise, was in the bottom 25% of all the teams in the state. But my father was the kind of coach who adjusted to his team; he knew with limited raw talent he had to rely upon execution to win. We went up against teams who should have destroyed us, but we excelled as a unit: no turnovers and no bad shots. He had us so fundamentally skilled on offense, sometimes we were absolutely machinelike. We loved walking onto the floor against big, brawny teams who were probably laughing under their breath, wondering how these little guys had made it so far. In the state championship game, we were so well prepared, my dad didn't even have to talk strategy in the huddles. He concentrated on motivation—

friends, loyalty, sweat—because we knew what plays to run. We were crazy with emotion, but still smooth and efficient. And we just wouldn't let each other down that day.

It's much more than championships, though. His style of coaching changed my life and the lives of many others. I strive to do my best in every single area of my life. In school I go for the best grades possible. When I'm in the world of work, I know I'll be hustling to be better than anyone else. But along the way, I'll appreciate the people around me. It's the loyalty I've mentioned already. He created an environment where I grew to love my teammates; to this day, I'd lay down my life for them. They'd do the same for me. I tell friends at college what it was like to be on that Northgate team, about what loyalty really means. At first they don't get it, but in time they see the way my dad taught me to walk through the world as I did through a basketball game: with respect, pride, loyalty, concentration, and teamwork. These will characterize my life forever and will take me wherever I want to go.

Here is what I'd like to say to my father: There isn't a day goes by that I don't think of our times together at home or at Northgate. You have totally prepared me for life. I'm ready right now for any challenge, any obstacle. Thanks.

FRANK ALLOCCO
*president, Incentives for Learning; basketball
coach at De La Salle High School*

— w r i t i n g   a b o u t —

DONALD CARPENTER
his high school football coach

Since the eighth grade, my goal had been to be quarterback at the University of Notre Dame. I had heard their games on the radio, watched them on television, and dreamed about the day I would play football for their legendary coach Ara Parseghian. When I was a sophomore on our high school team, I asked our backfield coach to give me drills to help me achieve my goal. He laughed, "You're not even starting *here*. How are you going to play football *there?*" But he agreed to help me after practice. Throughout my high school career, I worked late with Donald Carpenter, every day striving for the opportunity to play for Coach Parseghian.

I was named starting quarterback at New Providence High School my junior year. Our team finished with six wins and three losses, and we won five of our last six games. Coach Carpenter had earned my trust and confidence through our work both on and off the field. I learned he was a devout man with a sincere faith in doing the right thing. And he was an outstanding motivator; I was mesmerized by his stories and believed in his coaching methods.

I remember a game we were playing with Verona High

School—the number three team in the state of New Jersey. The game was a defensive battle that amply entertained the 6,000 fans. With four minutes to go, we had the ball and were driving toward the end zone. I went back to pass and just as I was releasing the ball, I was blindsided and fumbled it. Verona recovered the football. I staggered to the sidelines, upset I had cost my team an opportunity to win. When I reached Coach Carpenter, he asked me what I was crying about. I told him I had cost our team the game. He reminded me it wasn't over yet, that I had to maintain my faith, and that we would still get a chance to win. Four plays later, when Verona lined up for a winning field goal attempt, Coach Carpenter reached down to hold my hand and whispered, "Think fumble." Seconds later, their holder bobbled the snap and we recovered the ball. As I ran onto the field, I looked back at him in shock, thinking, *I hope now he's thinking touchdown pass.* Five plays later, with twenty-five seconds left in the game, I threw twenty yards to win the game. As my teammates and our fans celebrated ecstatically, I looked at him and thought how much I believed in that man.

When my junior year concluded, I led our county in yards passing and touchdown passes, and was named to the All-State team. That summer, I spent many hours with Coach Carpenter working on my passing and running skills. Before the beginning of my senior year, *Kickoff* magazine named me one of the top 100 backs in the country. That August, I received a letter from Coach Ara Parseghian informing me of Notre Dame's interest in me as a scholar-athlete. All my dreams were coming to fruition.

Our high school team looked impressive in preseason scrimmages my senior year. We defeated two perennial football powers in the state of New Jersey. I threw for five touchdowns against Union and ran for over 150 yards against Butler. I couldn't wait for the season to begin.

Finally, our first regular-season game arrived; we opened at home against Springfield High School. The stands were packed to watch New Providence's "Aerial Circus" roll. The first time we had a passing situation, I dropped back to pass, but then handed the ball to my younger brother Richard, who ran for thirty yards. I recall striding down the field to our next play, thinking what a special year this was going to be. Three plays later I threw my first touchdown pass of the new season.

After our defense held the opponent, I eagerly took the field again. On our second play, I rolled out to the right side and plowed into Springfield's defensive back. After the initial shock of the hit, I realized my shoulder wasn't feeling right. When I looked down, my left clavicle had been broken. I walked to the sidelines and desperately told Coach Carpenter I would only be out for a few minutes. The team doctor examined my shoulder as I lay on a bench. I knew my season was over when Coach Carpenter came over and started to cry. I remember weeping myself as the ambulance drove me away.

In the emergency room, my dad and my older brother Jerry tried to console me by telling me I would be healed in time for basketball season. Several hours later, as we left the hospital, my spirits had improved. However, as I turned on the radio, there was Notre Dame's fight song playing at the conclusion of another win. I cried more tears as I concluded that dream was over too. . . .

When I arrived home, most of my teammates were there to console me. I assured them I would do everything in my power to play again. When Coach Carpenter walked through the door, our eyes met and filled with tears. He sat down next to me and told me I had to believe, I had to stay positive, my dreams could still come true.

During the next few months, he sent films of those preseason scrimmages to Notre Dame. He wrote them about my overwhelming desire for the game and my extraordinary love for Notre Dame. In April, I was invited to visit the university and was offered a full scholarship to play football. It was the first time Notre Dame had offered a scholarship to a player who had not played his senior year of high school. A week later, Coach Carpenter along with my parents watched me sign my letter of intent accepting the scholarship offer. Once again, his message to have faith despite overwhelming odds, rang true.

Coach Donald Carpenter is still a physical education teacher and football coach at New Providence High School in New Jersey. He has coached side by side with Head Coach Frank Bottone for the past thirty-five years. Together they have built a football powerhouse that contends annually for state championship accolades. More importantly, Coach Carpenter has been a positive influence on the thousands of youngsters he has coached. I feel blessed I had the good fortune to learn lessons of faith, hope, loyalty, love, discipline, and dedication from this fine teacher at a time when I was developing my foundation for adult life.

I won three varsity letters at the University of Notre Dame and I played on the 1973 National Championship football team. Today I am a high school basketball coach at Northgate High School in Walnut Creek, California. I often think back to my years at New Providence High and realize my philosophy when working with young adults was molded by this inspirational teacher.

SARAH ALTMAN
medical student

— writing about —

VICKI HACKETT
her eleventh-grade English teacher

When Mrs. Vicki Hackett asked me to write a letter of support to the county selection committee for her possible selection as Teacher of the Year, I felt incredibly honored. A teacher I respect and admire was entrusting me with an important task. But as I sat down to write, my sense of pride was replaced by fear. I thought I would simply list all Mrs. Hackett's attributes, but I knew such a list would be a poor representation of the truth. Instead I want to tell you about my English class.

At first I assumed it was going to be a really long year; around me sat twenty-eight guys and, including Mrs. Hackett, only six other women. The class, held right after lunch, was loud and the students were not overly interested in the topic of American literature. Settling back into my chair, I began to write off another year of English. But when Mrs. Hackett walked up to the front of the room, I thought maybe I had judged too quickly.

Instead of aggressively taking control of the situation, she introduced herself and enthusiastically told us about the year she had planned for us—from Steinbeck to poetry to multi-cultural literature. She finished her introduction soliciting students' questions and comments. This first day was not some dramatic turnaround where my classmates suddenly became quiet, hard-working, and diligent, but it did set a stage for learning characterized by teamwork, mutual respect, and personal growth. Because of the respect Mrs. Hackett showed for others as well as the material she taught, students saw themselves as partners in their own education.

One of Mrs. Hackett's greatest strengths is her ability to treat everyone in her class as an individual; she recognizes we all have strengths and weaknesses, as well as incredibly diverse private lives. By highlighting people's talents, whether they were visual, oratory, or literary, Mrs. Hackett helped us seek our full potential and, as teams, do things better than we could ever have done alone. Through units like multi-cultural literature, we were encouraged to learn more about other cultures while simultaneously discovering more about our own.

The thing I treasure most about Mrs. Hackett's class was the freedom she gave me to learn about myself. We were given a personal reflective essay assignment, with the topic left open. I struggled for a long time about what I was going to write: Should I put my emotions on paper or just recall a pleasant experience from my past? Because of the trust I felt in Mrs. Hackett, I decided on the former—a highly emotional paper with the words "DO NOT SHOW TO ANYONE" written across the top.

Instead of simply critiquing the paper and returning it, Mrs. Hackett cared enough to talk with me about the topic, not as a teacher to a student, but as one person to another. I know I am not the only person who opened up to Mrs. Hackett. When she sees something wrong and asks if you want to talk, you know this is not a platitude, but an honest invitation.

Because of her commitment to me and to all her students, Mrs. Hackett moved beyond being just my junior English teacher and became my mentor and my friend. Looking back, I feel extremely fortunate to have been assigned to Mrs. Hackett's class. I sincerely hope this committee recognizes Mrs. Hackett's rare gifts, because I know they have made a tremendous difference in the lives of over 3,000 students, including my own.

VICKI HACKETT
high school English teacher, Mt. Diablo Teacher of the Year, 1996

— w r i t i n g   a b o u t —

CLAYTON WIGGINTON
her fourth-grade teacher

In 1954 I found myself in the classroom of my first male teacher. Mr. Wigginton created an unforgettable fourth-grade world for us, his lucky students. Dynamic, energetic, and caring, he immersed us in art, music, humanity, and concern for one another. We became a family of fourth graders, distinguished from the other classes by our eagerness to return to class—even after recess.

What made Mr. Wigginton so special? When we hurt or embarrassed ourselves, he supported us, enabling us to develop self-esteem and maturity. I clearly remember tickling Howard Snyder after reading group one day just to get his attention. I succeeded, but I embarrassed him too, and he cried. When Mr. Wigginton asked for the person who "bothered" Howard to stand up, I was paralyzed with humiliation; I could not stand. A few minutes later, he wisely ran a short movie and I quietly slipped back to his desk to admit my guilt. Rather than make my humiliation more intense, he helped me understand Howard's reaction, his embarrassment. Then Mr. Wigginton and I together thought of other, more socially acceptable ways to get Howard's attention. Here was a teacher who turned every situation in the classroom into a learning experience and I loved him for that. Now I realize what energy it takes to be patient, to reach for long-term learning rather than a short-term fix.

When we left him to become fifth graders, we all had mixed emotions: sadness to leave and eagerness to grow. Imagine my delight when my sixth-grade class assignment read "Clayton C. Wigginton." Early that year, we packed up all our school belongings and moved from the portables to our brand-new Biscayne Gardens Elementary School. We also attended the wedding celebration Mr. Wigginton held especially for us and the students of his new wife, our second-grade teacher. It was at his home, complete with hot dogs and a swimming pool. How special we felt when he wanted to share his new life with us.

We shared ours with him too: the good and the bad, the happy and the sad. When my grandmother died that year, I had trouble concentrating and sleeping because I was constantly trying to remember every detail of her home, down to the last periwinkle. He somehow discovered my inner grief and helped me to write and draw and take breaks from concentrating. He assured me I would never forget her, that I could relax and her memory would still be with me. This is a teacher who cared far more about me than about the curriculum.

I still remember certain lessons from that sixth-grade year; Mr. Wigginton made learning so interesting and fun we didn't recognize the hidden requisites. I realized then I wanted to do what Mr. Wigginton did: help students bring out the best in themselves, encourage them to contribute positively to the world, and make learning fun and meaningful. I wrote to Mr. Wigginton once when I was in college, telling him I was going to become a teacher; by then, he had become a principal. I remember hoping he still had plenty of contact with students, not realizing his encouragement of teachers would also have a great impact on many young people. I'd like him to know I have chosen my career wisely, that he was an excellent role model, and that I attribute my success and joy in this career to him.

Thank you, Mr. Wigginton, wherever you are.

JEFF FEINMAN
world traveler

— w r i t i n g   a b o u t —

JEFF SPODEN
his U.S. history teacher

I first heard of Jeff Spoden from my sister who was his student two years before I reached his classroom. Never one to revere authority or respect attendance policy, she seemed to contradict herself when confessing, "I'm scared to cut Spoden's class; he'll take it personally and I can't deal with the guilt." So when I first entered the room of the teacher with the John Lennon spectacles who slinked humbly down the hallway, I knew he was someone special.

On the first day—barely after we had entered the room—Mr. Spoden marched the entire class out of the high school and onto the football field. There he used the hundred-yard field as a historical time line for us to gain perspective on the immaturity of our young country.

"Where do you think the birth of Jesus Christ took place on this time line?" he asked. Several of us ran out to the forty-yard line to mark our spots.

"How about the extinction of the dinosaurs?"

"The writing of the Constitution?"

After running around for a while, we were eventually led to somewhere inside the one-yard line, just inches from the goal line, and thus gained a perspective on the "infant U.S.A." that none of us had had before.

In retrospect, that day we left the classroom was a symbol of what Spoden was trying to show us. Never before had a teacher encouraged us to look at ourselves and the world through the lenses of our own critical eyes. After all, we were young, fortunate kids weaned on the conservative values of the Reagan era. These values had never been challenged or debated; they had just slowly embedded themselves into our worldview. We had just accepted whatever canned information was thrown at us and then made plans for the weekend.

But with Spoden, my little perspective began to broaden. With his unconventional style, he knifed open history's imperious belly and freed us to see it as we wished. Now there wasn't just one way to read history—or watch the news, or view ourselves—there were hundreds. Before long, it became clear that to Spoden, creativity and critical thinking were just as important to learn as the facts of U.S. history.

He was an unapologetically left-leaning thinker, though not a dogmatic one. This wasn't always understood by parents. In fact, one year, some outraged parent, apparently feeling threatened by Spoden's individualism, accused him of propagating communism. The charge was sheer lunacy, and it did nothing but solidify his spot on our "cool teacher" roster.

The fact is, though his liberal flair was a conspicuous presence in our classroom, he clearly valued the opinions of the conservative faction of our class. He always encouraged everyone's participation in our lively classroom debates, and he gave conservative students the opportunity to sharpen their ideas on his respectful challenges. Our orientation didn't matter, only that we thought for ourselves. To do otherwise would contradict the lesson of responsible thinking he worked to instill in us.

Spoden was always doing crazy stuff; he transformed the classroom into a theater and we all eagerly anticipated what would come next from this goofy Thespian. There was the time when he littered the classroom with soiled napkins, half-eaten food, and other waste to simulate the effects of the Industrial Revolution on America's cities. Or the famous Dust Bowl presentation, where we all got powdered with flour blown across the room. Or the time when he ate a package of head cheese—a processed chunk of assorted cattle parts—at the start of a lecture. I'm actually not sure how the head cheese stunt tied into his lecture, but it stands out nonetheless.

Our class was a Coney Island freak show in comparison to the cookie-cutter learning environments I'd grown accustomed to. Friends who missed a classic "Spoden moment" grimaced at their bad luck and mumbled about transferring into his class.

For me, it was a liberating experience. Before taking his class, I'd always felt smothered by the prescribed "roles" a teenager could assume. I wasn't just a jock, or just a stoner, or just a nerd, but a combination of all three. This instinct never felt validated until meeting Spoden. He was a man who loved the poetry of the Beats and the fast break of the Los Angeles Lakers. He was a wise guy and a cynic, yet could cry in front of his students. In short, he defied swift judgment and rigid categorization. He taught me that not only could I choose how to interpret history and world events, I could also choose who I wanted to be as an individual. Just so long as this individual cares about the human race and has the guts to try head cheese, I'm sure Spoden would approve.

JEFF SPODEN
high school history teacher

— w r i t i n g a b o u t —

ANGUS WRIGHT
his college professor

My tribute is not warm and fuzzy. My mentor didn't care about me in a time of need, or support me in any way. In fact, for some reasons that were just and others that weren't, he came to actively dislike me. Out of defensiveness, I returned the ill will, and we had a decidedly lousy relationship. Instead, this story celebrates the limitless power of ideas, and the reality that ideas can be much more significant than any one or two or thousand minds they inhabit.

Despite my bittersweet memories about my mentor, I can't deny he changed my life as no other person ever did. He was the boulder that tumbled into the river of my intellect, altering the flow of my life forever. Along this new channel, created in the fall of 1976 at Sacramento State University, the water was much cleaner and the ideas much more profound. Things began to make sense.

They started to make sense by applying the formula I now have in large letters over my classroom's front chalkboard: Think, Question, Challenge. Dr. Angus Wright asked us to do this the very first day of International Environmental Problems. I walked into Angus' class a Kennedy liberal, passionate but confused, asking questions but not the right ones. This began to change within thirty minutes. He projected a slide and invited us to ask questions about it. "What would we need to know to really understand this picture?" he queried. (I can't even count the number of times I've used this same line in my own teaching.) It was an aerial photo of the southwestern United States and northern Mexico, in the area where the Colorado River crosses the border. The questions started basically enough, but were soon into the realm of real inquiry and understanding.

When class ended, I was both disturbed and amazed. Disturbed because I hadn't contributed much to the analysis; I wasn't skilled in thinking or analyzing. Amazed because I sensed that a window had just opened and a whole new landscape was forming in the distance. Soon it wouldn't be distant; it would be my life. The world had just become larger and smaller at the same time. Looking at an aerial photograph for ninety minutes had introduced me to water, land, dams, siltation, salinity, agriculture, politics, economics, culture, immigration, and imperialism. Big messy subjects, but comprehensible if one took the time to slow down, ask questions, and think.

This exercise was a micro-version of the entire class. We spent the next fifteen weeks looking at global environmental issues and attempting to identify the root causes. Deforestation: why? Overpopulation: why? Poor water quality: why? WHY, WHY, WHY? In this exploration, I learned some hard and ugly truths, but it was exhilarating. I learned that Third World forests are cut down not because of "native" ignorance, but because wealthy landowners and transnational corporations have wanted them cut down to graze cattle, which end up on North American and European tables. I was shocked to learn that every single country on earth has the capacity to feed its own population. Unfortunately, most of the world's arable land is used to grow cash crops—coffee, bananas, sugar, fruit, and flowers—thus reaping huge profits for a few. Meanwhile most peasants are forced onto marginally productive land, eventually to give up and move to poverty-ridden cities crowded with people just like them. I learned people starve not because of any physical limitation on food production, but because of an appallingly unjust distribution of wealth. When Francis Moore Lappe and Joseph Collins published *Food First*, their comprehensive, impeccably researched work on this very subject, Angus Wright's students were already acquainted with much of the material. Soon after its release, I remember him grumbling good-naturedly, "They wrote my book."

We continued our search for answers to intractable problems, with Angus as our guide. It was like digging up bones in the backyard. He showed us where and how to dig: what questions to ask, what to read, how to analyze and then ask again. Unearthed and alive, these ideas would rise up out of the muck and slap my face hard, dislodging many cherished beliefs I'd held about my country and world. I grew angrier but more impassioned with each discovery:

The "green revolution" that was supposed to wipe out hunger was a disaster. These "miracle" strains of seed were expensive and needed massive amounts of water, chemical fertilizer, and pesticides.

Foreign aid was a complete sham: the lion's share of it was earmarked for military purchases. U.S. tax dollars flowed to Third World generals who funneled it right back to American arms manufacturers. Economic aid was similarly tied to contracts with American firms, virtually none of it helping those in need.

Post-war peasant uprisings and wars of national liberation were fought because people with little or no political and economic power were hungry, angry, and sometimes desperate, not because communists were instigating trouble. As Isabel Letelier said, "We the people of the Third World do not need the Soviets to tell the Cubans to tell us that we are hungry."

From the halls of Montezuma to the halls of the International Monetary Fund, the United States rarely did anything to alleviate the grinding poverty of people the world over. In fact, Washington virtually always sided with the wealthy against the poor, landlords against peasants, tyrants against rebels. It sent troops, it sent spies, it sent guns and then more guns; it toppled democratically elected governments; it propped up repressive thugs. All this in the name of Cold War containment, but in the light of evidence, about something very different.

All the U.S. wars, military interventions, covert operations, assassinations, campaigns of destabilization, and buying of elections were much less about confronting the Soviet Union than about forcing a stable, orderly investment climate upon other nations. They were about putting people in power who would promote profitability, or removing from power those governments that wouldn't go along with the program. They were about putting down—violently if necessary—rebellions against this system of economic dependence and exploitation. The Cold War provided a dark, wide cloak behind which to fight with people of the Third World over control of land and resources.

Acquiring this information was a seminal experience in my life. In a class ostensibly about environmental issues, my world rebuilt itself. How could I be the same? Allegiances tarnished and priorities changed. I couldn't carry information such as this and not want to tell others. I immediately took on a double major in environmental studies and international affairs, desperately wanting to teach others what I had learned. Graduate school became my plan, with a Ph.D. and a professorship in international political economy my goals.

Unfortunately, my enthusiasm and vision were not matched by my commitment and follow-through. I got decent grades, but spent a lot of time socializing and engaging in that venerable seventies pastime: "getting my head together." I took incompletes in several classes and flaked out in other major ways as well. In the process, I led professors who had seen real potential in me, including Angus Wright, to conclude I was an academic fraud. Toss into the mix some personal conflicts that were part his fault and part my own, and we wound up with a bad relationship. I felt rejected and sad; I'm not sure if he felt anything.

Despite this unhappy ending, I look back on this man as a

powerful force to whom I'm eternally grateful. He gave me a river of ideas and information so vital to who I have become, I feel compelled to name these ideas quite specifically. Simply stating "he was a left-wing intellectual who helped me to think critically about the world" would render the reality of it bland and impotent. He helped me find words that symbolized monumental ideas. These hard, clear words, which twenty years ago cut a fresh canyon through my intellectual landscape, still carry a force for me; they rise and curl off my tongue in discussion, and off the page whenever I write. They are all he ever gave me, but they are much more than I can ever thank or repay him for.

I haven't seen or talked to Angus in twenty years. I assume he is nearing retirement, and I hope he's still throwing hard rain into the faces of young students such as I was. I want him to know seeds sprout in the most unlikely places; flowers shoot not merely from fertile soil, but from hardened earth and even rock. I use what he gave me every day of my life, passing it on to new generations and praying for just a little more light.

CATHERINE LEWIS
college student

— w r i t i n g   a b o u t —

LISA ORTA
her english professor

LITTLE REVOLUTIONS

The first time I saw the name of my teacher Lisa Orta, it was an unwelcome surprise. Just before graduation from high school, I asked my English teacher who to take classes from at the local community college. He recommended Mr. Fischer, so I arranged my schedule to be in his class.

I felt uneasy and afraid starting college. Mr. Fischer's freshman English class seemed something I could count on in a sea of unknowns. So when I went to the bookstore to buy my textbook, I was startled to see an unfamiliar name printed on the placards for my section number: ORTA. I hoped it was just a clerical error, but when I worked up the courage to ask about it, I learned Mr. Fischer had been promoted to division chairperson and thus some of his classes were now assigned to other teachers. Despite my anxiety, I tried to reassure myself everything happens for a reason: Maybe I needed to learn something from this ORTA.

As it turned out, I was right. The first college instructor I ever talked to outside of class was Ms. Orta. She was so quick to laugh in warm, rich tones during class, I didn't feel my usual angst about going to a teacher's office for help. That first time, I stayed for a whole hour, long after we had finished discussing my essay. During that visit, she introduced me to her office mate, Mr. Barber, and said, "We're trying to start a revolution in the English Department." This exemplifies how I think of Ms. Orta—her own little revolution.

In her classroom, the *process* of writing and editing was as important as the finished product, if not more so. Learning how to be a successful student was measured not in the attainment of a grade but in the possession of a balanced life from which excellence can grow. Ms. Orta cared about her students as whole people struggling with the unique concerns of student life. She showed us college success videos she herself was in years earlier when she had taught seminars, and gave us handouts with which to schedule our time.

Ms. Orta graded on a portfolio system: Essays were given copious comments and suggestions for improvement; but no letter grade was assigned until, after multiple revisions and trials in student editing groups, all essays were turned in as a portfolio. At the end of the semester, these portfolios were assessed as much for improvements as for inherent quality. I remember many activities that illustrated how to write, from the day we made poems out of phrases in magazines, to our discussion circles that elicited the critical thinking from which writing is born.

For me, our burgeoning friendship outside the classroom became more important than the lessons of the English language. I can't count how many times I saw the glow of Ms. Orta's lamp through the window in her office door and walked toward it for help or the simple joy of conversation. She was always lending me books to read ("Oh, you haven't read *Cold Sassy Tree*? Here, you'll love it!").

And when I decided I wanted to transfer to the University of California at Irvine, she helped me immeasurably with the process. Ms. Orta assuaged my irrational fears with anecdotes about her own experiences at U.C. Berkeley. She read countless drafts of my application essay and then subsequent scholarship essays. During these sessions, I learned how to express myself within the confines of imposed structure. Ms. Orta understood the restrictions of form, content, and length intrinsic to such application essays but still knew exactly how to help me express my unique story. She wrote a letter of recommendation for my scholarship applications full of eloquent praise that I believe played a large part in my winning two substantial awards.

It has been two years since I first walked into Lisa Orta's classroom. The community college I was afraid to go to became a place I loved so much I took summer school just so I could postpone my departure. Mostly I didn't want to leave the comfort of following that light to her office whenever I needed help finding my voice.

One day after my acceptance to U.C. Irvine, I stood in her office and wondered aloud how I could ever repay her for all she had given me. Ms. Orta looked me straight in the eye and said matter-of-factly, "Catherine, this is what teachers live for."

LISA ORTA
English instructor

— w r i t i n g   a b o u t —

MRS. BENNETT
her kindergarten teacher

PRIMARY COLORS

I based my choice of profession—to be a teacher—on the single, simple act of finger-painting. It was 1960 in Mountain View, California. I was five years old and already an alumni of an elementary school in Burbank. All I can remember about my first kindergarten class was the teacher insisted on my writing with my right hand. I remember cold, shiny linoleum floors, our teacher's swishy, stiff skirt, her bright red lipstick stuck in a fake smile, and the nagging feeling I would never get it right.

Imagine my thrill when, relocated to the Bay Area, my mother marched me into Mrs. Bennett's classroom. Her pink sweater askew, she was sitting in one of our little chairs listening, enraptured, to one of the children report on his weekend. Interrupted by our tardy appearance, she looked up to greet me with a smile that told me I was home.

Everything about Mrs. Bennett was perfect—she sang with us in a weak, untrained falsetto, the way she lowered her voice to a whisper when she wanted our attention, the way she gave each one of us a chance to recite the alphabet and the Pledge of Allegiance in turn. Mrs. Bennett never allowed any child to exhibit impatience or scorn at another child's rate of learning or personal style. Each day after our morning lessons we would sit in a circle and she would call on us in turn. We were to say what activity we wanted to do for the next hour. There were lots of choices; Mrs. Bennett's classroom was always a bustle of noise and excitement. But there was only one thing I ever wanted to do and Mrs. Bennett let me do it every single day of kindergarten.

It wasn't just the gooey, messy quality of finger-painting that was such a thrill; it was the collusion it implied. Mrs. Bennett knew I struggled with my shyness, my left-handedness, my buck teeth, my sale-rack clothes, and especially my tremulous home life. She knew I didn't want to share or negotiate or converse with anyone. At the finger-painting table you got to work alone, in silence. While she gently prodded the other children to rotate through the various stations, she feigned surprise each day when I said, "Finger-paint." Then she made sure there was room for me at the back table. On the days no other child wanted to finger-paint, she never made a fuss about getting the paints out just for me. I remember the warm pressure of a kind hand on my shoulder.

And on open-school night Mrs. Bennett made like I was the best, the most accomplished kindergarten student she had ever had in her lifelong teaching career. In front of my parents she was quite an actress. She seemed to forget how painfully shy I really was, how my struggle to find self-worth and self-affirmation was such a daunting task for a mere five-year-old. To hear her talk, my virtues were countless, my academic accomplishments superior, my personality outgoing and engaging. My parents were to be proud and honored to live with such a precious and precocious child.

For all of their awkwardness at parenting and rocky times with each other, thanks to Mrs. Bennett, my parents never doubted my academic ability or effort. Mrs. Bennett showed me that she had the power to instill respect. It was the most significant and enduring gift of my childhood.

When I was in second grade, my family moved to a newly built house in Los Altos, a much more fancy neighborhood in the foothills. From then until her retirement nine years later, I visited Mrs. Bennett every year in June, my birthday month, to say thank you. She always greeted me with a hug that felt just right; she never forgot my name or my story. In her presence, even at age sixteen, I felt wanted and understood.

As I write this, I realize her story is now my story. I grew up to become a teacher and carry her lessons deep within me. I have taught high school English in the inner city; I've taught reading and writing and communication skills to adults in various industries; and now I teach English at Diablo Valley College, a suburban community college. There are days when decisions about lessons and books and course selections overwhelm me. And then I find myself remembering that the content of what I teach isn't the most important aspect of my job. My job as a teacher is to help students know that, if necessary, they can finger-paint over and over again on the road to healing. My job is to carry on the work of Mrs. Bennett, to guide students to the magical place of self-respect because that is where all learning takes place.

Honor Your Most Influential Teacher

The Teacher Appreciation Project is an ongoing project devoted to honoring individual teachers, coaches, and other mentors. Our plan is to publish another volume of tributes just like this one, and we would love for you, as either purchaser or recipient of this book, to submit a story or poem about your most influential mentor.

Your tribute should paint a picture of who this person is and why they were so important to you. How did they challenge you, soothe you, or drive you to greater accomplishments? What important lesson did they teach you about a subject or about life? Use anecdotes to show how this took place.

Stories should be no more than 1,500 words; poems should not exceed 50 lines. All submissions must be typed. Please include your name, address, phone number, fax number, and e-mail address. Submit to:

Jeff Spoden / Teacher Appreciation Project
c/o Andrews McMeel
4520 Main Street
Kansas City, MO 64111-7701

Jeff Spoden has taught high school social studies for thirteen years. Spoden is also a music and movie enthusiast and an avid follower of local, national, and global politics. He lives in Walnut Creek, California, with his wife and two children.